Picture
Personalities

Picture Personalities

§

THE EMERGENCE OF THE STAR SYSTEM IN AMERICA

Richard deCordova

Foreword by Corey K. Creekmur

UNIVERSITY OF ILLINOIS PRESS
Urbana and Chicago

For my mother, Frances deCordova,
and in memory of my father, Jack deCordova

First paperback edition, 2001
© 1990, 2001 by the Board of Trustees
of the University of Illinois
Manufactured in the United States of America
P 6 5 4 3

∞ This book is printed on acid-free paper.

Library of Congress Cataloging-in-Publication Data
deCordova, Richard, 1956–1996
Picture personalities : the emergence of the star system in
America / Richard deCordova.
p. cm.
Includes bibliographical references and index.
ISBN 10: 0-252-07016-X (pbk. : alk. paper)
ISBN 13: 978-0-252-07016-7
1. Motion picture industry—United States—History.
2. Motion picture actors and actresses—United States.
3. Motion picture studios—United States.
I. Title.
PN1995.62.D43   1990
791.43'.028'0973—DC20   89-24739
                              CIP

University of Illinois Press
1325 South Oak Street
Champaign, IL 61820-6903
www.press.uillinois.edu

Contents

Foreword

Corey K. Creekmur

In this admirably compact book, the late Richard deCordova (1956–96) seamlessly merged two of the most significant projects in recent film studies, the return to early film history and the cultural analysis of the movie star. His generation of film scholars began thoroughly questioning the received wisdom on these topics in order to effectively demonstrate that the origins of cinema, the exemplary form of modern mass culture, had been inadequately addressed and incompletely chronicled.

Led by Richard Dyer's groundbreaking *Stars* (1979), younger researchers also conducted the first careful investigations of the movie star, who functioned simultaneously as sign, social type, fetish, and commodity. Scholars willing to acknowledge the cultural significance of stars soon extended their discussions to the larger culture of celebrity, fame, and fandom. Once an embarrassment to serious film criticism, fans are now analyzed as carefully as the stars they worship, and deCordova's book played a notable role in directing that shift in critical attention.

Although most earlier film histories had included a brief account of the movie star's "invention" and the gradual development of the "star system" for grooming, training, and promoting performers, this story had never been accurately told, as deCordova shows with efficiency in his opening pages. Previous historical accounts had in fact often resembled the stories Hollywood enjoys telling about itself: real talent always shines through, hard work always pays off, and anyone, no matter how humble (or foreign) their origins, can become a star. In addition to popular backstage glimpses in movies like *Show People* (1928), *What Price Hollywood?* (1932), and its three remakes as *A Star Is Born* (1937, 1954, and 1976),

Hollywood also told the public its "inside" story through the fan magazines that focused almost exclusively on the (studio-approved) private lives of stars. As deCordova traces with care, the early audience's keen interest in "personalities" would eventually turn to a lurid fascination with the scandals that transformed the image and self-regulation of Hollywood before the arrival of sound.

Picture Personalities remains, more than a decade after its publication, an invaluable and unsurpassed account of a crucial transformation in film history and modern culture. DeCordova's work paved the way for influential later studies of early Hollywood, such as Miriam Hansen's *Babel and Babylon: Spectatorship in American Silent Film* (1991) and Gaylyn Studlar's *This Mad Masquerade: Stardom and Masculinity in the Jazz Age* (1996). DeCordova's analysis of the American star system has been extended by scholars interested in European, Asian, and Latin American popular cinemas as well. An example of the most productive kind of scholarship, *Picture Personalities* brought what had been an incomplete investigation to a precise conclusion while providing a rigorous model for later work. A reissue of this book is therefore especially welcome since the work it engendered is still visibly underway.

Sadly, *Picture Personalities* must now also serve as a promise of the future work its author would have produced. Before its publication, Richard deCordova had already written insightful essays in film theory, and following this book's appearance he began research on Hollywood's construction of children as an audience. The essays he published on this topic are typically balanced between archival evidence and wide-ranging ideas: they were certainly instrumental in the development of an interest in children's culture (rather than the more common youth culture centered on adolescents) in current media studies.

Richard deCordova's death robbed his wife, Susan, their children, Jacob and Emily, and his large number of friends and professional admirers of his joyful presence and exceptional generosity. It's a small but hardly insignificant comfort that this book, the first accurate account of its important subject, will keep his name alive in film scholarship, to which he devoted his professional life. I hope the spirit of the very bright and kind man who wrote it might also continue to inspire future readers and students with its equal measure of love for the movies and desire to get things right.

Acknowledgments

I am pleased to be able to express my appreciation to those people who have helped me in various ways in the completion of this project. My work on the early star system began as a dissertation project at UCLA, and the members of my committee—Nick Browne, Janet Bergstrom, Teshome Gabriel, Bertrand Augst, and Thomas Hines—had an important and formative influence on much that is contained here. Nick Browne and Janet Bergstrom deserve special thanks for their encouragement and support and for the close, critical readings they provided.

A number of people read this manuscript at one or more of its various stages and provided helpful and detailed criticism: Robert C. Allen, David Desser, Susan Freedman, Virginia Wright Wexman, Dana Polan, Roberta Pearson, and Ben Singer. I owe these people more of a debt than my thanks here can repay, but of course I thank them all. David Desser also provided the title suggestion, for which I am grateful.

Portions of this work have been presented at the Workshop on Mass Culture at the University of Chicago, at the Institute for Cinema and Culture at the University of Iowa, and at the Mass Culture Theory Study Group of the Center for Interdisciplinary Research in the Arts at Northwestern University. I thank Loren Kruger, Lauren Rabinovitz, Dudley Andrew, and Mimi White for the invitations and the participants in these sessions for their thoughtful comments and questions.

This book was made possible, in part, by two grants from DePaul University. I would like to thank the University Research Council and its head, Richard Yanikoski, and the College of Liberal Arts and Sciences and its dean, Richard J. Meister, for the much-needed and much-appreciated support. I would also like to thank the chairs of the Communication and English Departments, Richard Katula and Jim Malek, and, more generally, all of my colleagues at DePaul for providing such a pleasant and productive environment while I worked on this book.

A number of libraries and archives have been instrumental in providing access to the historical materials upon which this study is based. I would like to thank the staffs of the UCLA Theater Arts Library, The Margaret Herrick Library of the Academy of Motion Picture Arts and Sciences, The New York Public Library Theater Arts Collection, The Motion Picture Division of the Library of Congress, The Indiana State Library, The Los Angeles County Museum of Natural History, and the Hoblitzelle Theatre Arts Collection at the University of Texas for their generous assistance. Mary Corliss at the Film Stills Archive of the Museum of Modern Art and the staffs of the Library of Congress and the New York Public Library were also extremely helpful by assisting me in locating the photographs that appear here.

Finally, I would like to thank my mother, who has provided not only unending encouragement and assistance, but also a model for how to live a productive and joyous life.

Introduction

Aᴌᴛʜᴏᴜɢʜ individual films exist without stars it is difficult to imagine a cinema without them—an American cinema at least. The star system has been central to the functioning of the American cinema as a social institution, yet until recently there has been very little serious work done on movie stars. The large body of material about them has been anecdotal and uncritical, not far removed from the copy produced by press agents and devoured so readily by the media. This is almost as evident in discussions of the emergence of the star system as it is in the "exposés" of the "real lives" of the stars that we see daily in magazines and on television. Yet the emergence of the star system qualifies, by all accounts, as an important social phenomenon. Within the space of a very few years there was a transition from a cinema completely without stars to a cinema wholly dependent on them. Why did the star system emerge, and how has it affected the development of the cinema as an institution?

Most writers on the star system have asked these questions about its origin, but none have done the research or employed the methodological precision necessary to answer them properly. Without this research the star "histories" remain facile, oversimplified tales based on the overblown claims of film manufacturers and publicity agents. Frank E. Woods's 1919 article in *Photoplay* "Why Is a Star?" was probably the first attempt at a history of the star system.[1] Woods had been an active force in the development of the cinema to that point, having founded the moving picture section of the *New York Dramatic Mirror* and gone on to become a scenario writer at Biograph and chief assistant to D. W. Griffith at Mutual. At the time the article appeared he worked as the supervising director of Famous Players. His history of the star consists largely of his "reminiscences" and the reported conversations of an imaginary public. Most of his assertions have been accepted by later writers as fact and used as the basis for histories of the early star system.

Woods argued that public curiosity was the force that created the star system. The public wanted to know the names of the figures they saw on the screen, but the manufacturers wanted to "avoid the troubles of the theatrical managers—big salaries to stars and players—by rigidly concealing the names of the players."[2] The public responded by giving names to the players they liked and then demanding them. The Vitagraph Girl and the Biograph Girl were the first stars in this account. Their rise to stardom was accomplished without the aid of the manufacturers. Woods gave himself a very important place in this history. Moving picture fans wrote to Woods at the *Dramatic Mirror* asking about specific players in films. He answered the letters, and after that, the lid was off. According to Woods, Kalem was the first company to yield to the public demand for stars, and Vitagraph soon followed. Biograph, however, refused to release the names of its stars. Florence Lawrence and her successor, Mary Pickford, never received billing while at Biograph. Finally, after Lawrence, Pickford, and others had left Biograph and achieved fame elsewhere, Biograph capitulated and began rereleasing its films with these stars.

Terry Ramsaye, in 1925, gave an influential and quite different account of the emergence of the star system.[3] He argued that Carl Laemmle began the star system as a means of challenging the domination of the Motion Picture Patents Company (MPPC), an alliance of manufacturers that had banded their patents together in an attempt to gain total control of the industry. Laemmle lured Florence Lawrence, the "Biograph Girl," away from Biograph to join his Imp Company and, through a clever publicity stunt, turned her into a star. He planted an article in the *St. Louis Post-Dispatch* claiming that Lawrence had been killed. The next day, according to Ramsaye,

Lawrence appeared, "in person on the stage to let the world know that 'The Biograph Girl' was now an Imp."[4]

Benjamin Hampton's *A History of the Movies*, published in 1931, can be seen as an attempt to reconcile the two previous accounts. Hampton, like Ramsaye, claims that the star system emerged out of an opposition between the Patents Trust and the Independents. He does not place as much emphasis on the personal initiative of Carl Laemmle, however, viewing the opposition instead in terms of a broad thematic that runs throughout his book. Hampton argues that the Trust members were dedicated to a factory system that opposed progress, creativity, and the public's desire, while the Independents aimed at giving the public precisely what it wanted. This latter strategy worked in the Independents' favor, since by following it, they discovered the intensity of the public's desire for stars. They capitalized on this desire and the star system was born. Hampton claims that Mary Pickford was the first star, and he credits the Imp company with making her name known to the public. The Trust, meanwhile, predictably hesitated to acknowledge the new phenomenon. This is seen as a decisive miscalculation in their battle with the Independents.

Hampton stops short of claiming that the Independents were responsible for the creation of the star system, though. He finally disavows their role as anything more than a passive cooperation by claiming that the public created the star system:

> To imply that the independent producers sensed the deep interest of the public in movie personalities, and created the star system because of their superior acuteness, while General Film manufacturers were obtuse, would entirely misrepresent the situation. The fact is that the almost hysterical acceptance of personality exploitation by movie-goers was a startling surprise to all factors and all factions in the screen world. No one had foreseen it, and no one was in any degree prepared for the results that followed its advent. The star system in films was in reality created by the public, and the

public has had full and undisputed charge of its creation during every moment.[5]

This appeal to the public's desire as the prime determinant of the star system is very much in line with Woods's argument, of course. Although Hampton provides an elaborate treatise on the stakes of the Trust wars and the functioning of the public's desire, his only contention that deviates from the earlier histories is that Mary Pickford was the first star.

Lewis Jacobs, in *The Rise of the American Film* (1939), gives a slightly more detailed version of Ramsaye's account.[6] He sees the star system as a direct outcome of the Independents' battle with the Trust, and sees Laemmle's promotion of Florence Lawrence as the initiatory act. Jacobs provides some information that throws Ramsaye's dates into question. According to Jacobs, the death report was circulated well before (not the day before) Lawrence's appearance in St. Louis. Jacobs admits that some of the Trust members (Vitagraph, Lubin, Kalem) at some point adopted the star policy, but he leaves the specifics of this to the reader's imagination and goes on to discuss Biograph, the last of the companies to advertise its stars.

Alexander Walker's *Stardom: The Hollywood Phenomenon* contains the most thorough version of this story.[7] Walker provides the first reasonably accurate account of the sequence of events that constituted the Laemmle/Lawrence promotion. His revision of previous histories is primarily one of detail; he accepts the general framework offered by Ramsaye and Hampton. However, he makes two points that are significant additions to the standard accounts. First, he claims that Lawrence was not secured by Laemmle through a raid on Biograph. In fact, Lawrence was out of work at the time because she had been blacklisted by the MPPC manufacturers for trying to negotiate a better contract with Essanay. Unfortunately, Walker fails to provide any evidence for this assertion, nor does he mention his sources. The second point he makes is that the manufacturers were not alone in resisting the star system; the players themselves did not want their names revealed because they did not consider acting in the moving pictures a legitimate profession. This was certainly a prominent excuse for not revealing the players' names between 1910 and 1912, one that deserves consideration.

All of the major film histories (Jowett, Knight, Mast, Sklar, Cook) and treatments of stars (Dyer, Schickle) rely completely on these sources and accept their mode of historical explanation. Gorham Kindem's recent study, "Hollywood's Movie Star System: A Historical Overview," adds a couple of references to previously un-consulted sources, but stays within the general framework of these accounts.[8]

Anthony Slide's short article, "The Evolution of the Film Star," is to some degree outside of this tradition.[9] The only secondary source that Slide seems to rely on is Robert Grau's *Theater of Science*. He appeals to Grau and to his own research to challenge two aspects of the standard account of the emergence of the star system. First, he argues that the early film actors were not actually concerned about the legitimacy of their profession or their theatrical reputation. The actors were in reality (according to Grau) members of provincial stock companies who had no reputation to lose and who were, in many cases, desperate for work. Slide claims that there were no complaints from the Kalem players when their names were revealed to the public in January 1910. Slide's second point is that the Biograph players' names were known to the public by 1912, well before the company changed its policy in 1913 and "officially" released them. Slide points to several articles before 1913 that mention the names of the Biograph players.

Slide's presentation of original research is commendable, but the facts that he puts forward have little explanatory power in them-selves. The explanation offered by the classic film histories remains fundamentally unchallenged. This explanation basically proposes a series of four "events":

1. The public wanted to know the names of the performers.
2. The producers resisted revealing the performers' names for two reasons. First, they did not want to pay higher salaries to

performers, and second, the performers were in reality legitimate actors who would risk their reputations by appearing by name in films.

3. Carl Laemmle, in a move designed to gain an ascendancy over the Motion Picture Patents Company, introduced the first star, Florence Lawrence. The star system thus emerged out of a struggle between Trust members and Independents.

4. The Independents and the public finally won and the star system was born.

There is good reason to suspect the accuracy of many of these points, but whether accurate or not, this series of events hardly stands as an adequate historical explanation. The narrative logic of this account eludes all of the questions that would seek a more complex logic in the rise of the star system. A good simple story is the result, one that has lent itself to frequent repetition. Unfortunately, the emergence of the star system is not so simple. A number of objections to the standard account must be raised. Some concern the accuracy of its evidence, others its mode of historical explanation.

Woods and Hampton (and other historians to a lesser extent) posit the public's desire as the prime determinant of the star system. The question they never ask is, "Where did the public's desire come from?" Desire is seen as a reified force outside of all social determination. By appealing to it as the cause of the star system these historians effectively eliminate all consideration of the material practices that in some way formed the public's desire for movie stars.

The ideological thrust of this type of explanation is clear in the following passage from Hampton: "as soon as the star system appeared on the screen the consumer had thrown the manufacturer and the exhibitor out of the driver's seat and . . . ever thereafter the whimsical, mercurial, merciless populace would decide the course its entertainment should follow."[10] For Hampton, the emergence of the star system is the event that proved the democratic basis of the cinematic institution. The audience created stars by voting for its favorite actors at the box office, and in doing so it asserted both its freedom from and its control over the production process. This is a problematic view. What Hampton fails to acknowledge is that desire is in no way outside of the production process. It does not arise out of thin air, unsolicited. Nowhere is this more evident than in the machinery that emerged to produce and popularize the movie star.

The contention that the players' names were concealed is based largely on the assumption that it would have been natural for the names to be revealed much earlier. The resistance to the star should not be ascribed so much to the stubbornness of manufacturers as to the prevailing view of the film commodity before 1907. To accuse the manufacturers of concealing names at that time is like accusing Ford of not revealing the names of the people who assembled your car. Yet, arguments for the concealment theory tend to be based on the fact that the revelation of names happened gradually, not overnight, and that Biograph seemed to have refused to reveal its players' names until 1913.

There is little doubt that the shift in the commodity and enunciative status of film disrupted the previous business practices of the manufacturers. The argument that the manufacturers were worried about the potential escalation of players' wages cannot be dismissed—but neither can the increased commercial viability of the film emphasizing the star. Standard accounts would almost lead one to believe that the industry entered into the star system against its will, but this is not at all the case. A reassessment of the manufacturers' place in this history is obviously needed.

The argument that the players were partially responsible for the concealment of their names because of their theatrical reputations is difficult to sustain. One can imagine that many players had theatrical ambitions and felt cheapened by posing in moving pictures, but the events that led to the emergence of the star system worked to their advantage since it legitimized film acting as both an art and a profession. While it is true that film actors did not demand publicity before 1910, one should not conclude from this that they shunned it. Their anonymity was the result of a particular system of production (and reception) that prevailed at the time. This system of production, and the actor's role within it, changed drastically between 1907 and 1912.

There is no evidence to suggest that the actors actively resisted this change.

Jeanne Allen has demonstrated that the opposition between the Motion Picture Patents Company members and the Independents was not nearly as clear-cut as previous historians have suggested.[11] Allen argues that the Independents' role in both the rise of the feature film and the movement of production to California has been greatly exaggerated and offers evidence of the Trust members' early involvement in both of these areas.

A similar objection can be made to the standard accounts of the emergence of the star system. The contention that the Trust members resisted revealing the names of their players while the Independents fervently publicized theirs is easily disproved. The Edison Company publicized the appearance of Miss Cecil Spooner and Mademoiselle Pilar-Morin in 1909 in the trade press. Kalem released a poster of its players for lobby display in January 1910, two months before Laemmle's famous stunt. A Vitagraph poster appeared in April, and the promotion of Florence Turner—which was comparable to the Lawrence promotion in scope—began. Obviously, the Trust members were not lax in their capitalization on the personalities of their players.[12] Biograph is the only exception here, and it seems that film history has based its entire description of the Trust's star policy on this example.

This reassessment of the opposition between the Patents Trust and the Independents puts the claim that Carl Laemmle founded the star system into question. But this is not to say that J. Stuart Blackton of Vitagraph or Sigmund Lubin of Lubin started the star system. It is a mistake to reduce the determinations of the star system to the initiative of a single individual or even a single firm. The star was not dreamed up by an extraordinary individual with great foresight. A theory of history that assumes this must ignore the complexity of the conditions that made the star system possible—and desirable—at a given time.

Many studies of the phenomenon of stardom, and most popular writing, situate their analyses at the level of the individual star.

Such qualities as charisma, beauty, exceptional talent, and luck become the determinants of stardom. The opposing view sees stardom as the result and the product of a vast machinery referred to as the star system. It should be clear from my previous statements that I give more credence to this latter view. There is a danger of taking this position to the extreme, however, of viewing the system in terms that are too reductive and mechanistic. The star system does not produce stars the way that a factory produces goods. The system is rationalized, but it is not geared toward producing a standardized product in the usual sense of the word. It produces a product that is in fact highly individuated—the individual star. Images of machinery and the production line when applied to the star system may in some ways be appropriate, but they risk oversimplifying the processes that work to produce the star as individual entity.

The individual star has an undeniable specificity. The star's physical image is distinguishable from that of all other stars; the circulation of that image takes a historically specific course (through films, magazines, etc.) as do the statements that refer to the star. All gather to give the image a depth, a set of personality traits that, whether fictional or not, represent the star as individual. It is this specificity that makes the division between the individual star and the star system meaningful.

Roland Barthes has demonstrated the way in which this division operates in the popular reception of film and fan magazines. He argues that the central paradox of the star is that it is seen as both a person and an institution. Viewed as a person the star tends to elicit a positive response of sympathy. Viewed as the product of an institution or system, however, the star elicits a negative response (that Barthes says stems from the distaste we attach to any mechanization of the world). For Barthes, this allows the fan to contest the system at certain points and wholly deny its existence at others. This possibility is an integral part of the system itself. "Through star-making society imposes a strong tension which permits the fan to consume stars without however dignifying the processes which produce them."[13] The appeal of the star does indeed seem magical and highly individual. But the individuality of the star is never irreducibly outside of the star system since the system is geared toward producing just such individuality. The attempts by some stars to gain more control over their image or the resistance of others to the "machinery" itself is not unimportant. I do not want to slight these efforts, but neither do I want to turn them into an argument for the autonomy of stars from the system in which they are inscribed. The star who shuns stardom is as much a type today as the blond bombshell, and one that meets with much less resistance from the public, since such a star gives the illusion of being a real individual outside of the system.

Typically, the individual qualities and actions of the star (whether real or trumped up by press agents) enter quite readily into the system of discourse whose primary purpose is to differentiate stars while keeping knowledge about them within certain bounds. Lois Weber's statement that she likes automobiles, Anita King's identification with feminism, Florence Lawrence's appearance in St. Louis, Mary Pickford's divorce and her marriage to Douglas Fairbanks, Fatty Arbuckle's alleged rape of Virginia Rappe—all of these actions work to represent the star as individual (though each is figured at a much different level of generality). Only the latter action was so "individual" that the star system could not accommodate it, could not turn it around and use it as a selling point (although there were certainly efforts to do so). It is not surprising that this ended Arbuckle's tenure as a star. He could still speak, no doubt, but he could no longer "be spoken" by the system that had produced him as a star.

In this study I will take the star system as my object, not the individual star. Only through an examination of the full range of practices that constituted movie stars can one understand their emergence and functioning between 1907 and the early twenties. The individual star is the product of these practices, the result of a particular implementation of the star system. The individual who is the star may indeed have private, "individual" thoughts and feelings, but these only enter the public sphere as they are channeled through the star system and subjected to its requirements. The difficulty, as I see it, is in coming to grips with a system that is both systematic and individualizing. Two dangers must be avoided in this regard: one should neither oversimplify the systematic component by arguing that all stars come out of the same mold, nor exaggerate the extent to which the individual can be autonomous from the system that speaks him or her.

It is not surprising that the star system seems much more amorphous and indistinct than its product, the individual star. The star system is made up of both discursive practices and economic practices. This book will focus principally on the discursive organization of the star system, but one of the points that will clearly emerge from my arguments will concern the connection between the symbolic and economic identities of the star. The star could become the point of an economic exchange only by virtue of its identity as constructed in discourse. Thus, as the argument presented here will demonstrate, the star simultaneously changed the status of film as discourse and commodity.

The discursive organization of the star system is comprised of both a set of positions from which statements about stars can emerge and the statements themselves. An examination of the former leads to a description of the institutional and enunciative apparatus through which the star is produced. The positions from which statements about stars emerge are multiple, and each may diverge from the rest in its institutional setting or formal conventions. But each participates in the production of a common object—the star. These positions taken together form the most stable and systematic aspect of the star system.

The most fundamental perhaps is the position laid out for the actor in the fiction film. We call stars movie stars no doubt because of the primary importance we attach to their appearance in films (we do not call them magazine stars). This appearance not only allows for the most widespread and regularized circulation of the star's physical image, it also works to figure the star as subject of the discourse within which he or she is inscribed. The fictional status of the subjectivity that is thus represented is unimportant. The point to be made is that the cinema as an institution and as an enunciative form produces this position from which the star can speak and be spoken.

It produces others as well, of course—posters and song slides, which accompany the exhibition of films, personal appearances, and letters and photographs sent out to fans who write to the studio. These may not be as semiotically rich as the films, but they are nevertheless an integral and specific part of the apparatus through which stars are represented.

Journalism provided the institutional setting for much, if not most, of the discourse on stars. The trade press, fan magazines, the popular press, and newspapers all constituted specific positions from which to speak the star. The publications with the closest links to the cinematic institution—the trade press and fan magazines—were the most regular in their promulgation of stars. Articles in national magazines (such as *The Century* and *Woman's Home Companion*) and in local newspapers were more intermittent, but they undoubtedly reached a larger audience.

These discursive practices produce the star's identity, an identity that does not exist within the individual star (the way we might, however naively, believe our identities exist within us), but rather in the connections between and associations among a wide variety of texts—films, interviews, publicity photos, etc. The star's identity is intertextual, and the star system is made up in part of those ongoing practices that produce the intertextual field within which that identity may be seized by curious fans.

Of course the star system is also made up of the specific statements that emerge from those practices during a given period. The star system can be spoken of as such not only because the promotional identity-producing apparatus is made up of a number of distinct but interrelated parts, but also because of the systematic nature of the discourse produced through those parts. That discourse is extremely conventionalized. What can be said about those who appear in films at a given time fits into identifiable patterns and falls within specifiable bounds. The regularities and limits of star discourse constitute a crucial aspect of the star system as such. Thus, this study will concern itself both with the emerging apparatus of the star system and the emerging conventions for representing the identities of those who appear in films.

What do we "consume" when we go to the cinema? We consume a story, certainly, but not a story that could be recounted by a friend or summarized in prose to the same effect. Our experience of film is tied more to the specific telling of the story than to the abstract result of that telling, the story told. Our pleasure, in short, follows from our engagement in the film as process.

In recent years film studies has borrowed the concept of enunciation from linguistics in its consideration of these representational processes. The term refers simply to the act of producing a statement as distinct from the end result of that act, the statement produced (the enounced). The distinction is an important one. To analyze an enunciation is not to extract a meaning from a given statement or even to ascribe it a structure; it is, rather, to examine the activity of the statement's production.

Although a number of different aspects of film have been addressed in terms of enunciation (authorship, spectatorial position, etc.), the actor/star's role in the cinema's enunciative apparatus has been largely ignored. Yet it is clear that the actor figures prominently in the film's production of meaning. It would be a mistake to view the actor/star merely as a signifier (an enounced). The pleasure and the process of the American film has in fact been dependent on the assumption that actors hold a productive, transitive relation to their images on the screen. Historically, pronouncements about acting have probably been the most habitual, "natural" response to any inquiry about the quality or effectiveness of a film's construction. The actor's activity, in short, has been a principal category through which audiences have read, judged, and appreciated films.

Emile Benveniste's work in linguistics has provided the most influential model for considerations of enunciation in film.[14] Benveniste set out to describe the ways that language can signify and refer to its own production. This line of inquiry led Benveniste to delineate a "formal apparatus" of the enunciation in language, an apparatus composed primarily of verbal tense, shifters (here/there, this/that) and certain pronominal forms (I/You). Each of these aspects of language achieves its meaning only through reference to the instance of the statement's production.

Benveniste's analysis of the appearance and the positioning of the speaking subject in discourse has been his most important contribution in this area. This subject conventionally refers to the individual (or other agent) who produced the statement and who is therefore exterior to it. From another, more analytical perspective, however, the subject is that position in language that an individual must occupy to produce a given statement. One can, in a sense, become subject only in language and only through the constraints of the linguistic base. Proceeding from this insight, Benveniste attempts to outline the forms in which the subject can appear in language.

The most obvious example of these forms is the pronoun *I*. Benveniste demonstrates that "I" does not refer to external reality the same way that a noun does, or the way the pronoun *he* does. It refers fundamentally to the act of enunciation. "'I' can only be identified by the instance of discourse that contains it and by that alone," he states. "It has no value except in the instance in which it is produced." In other words, it has meaning only as one attends to the scene of the statement's production. The "I" appears as subject, as agent, in that scene.

This brief account of Benveniste's work may begin to reveal the concept of enunciation's pertinence to the analysis of artistic works, at least those works that depend primarily on language. Theories of literary narrative have, for instance, long attempted to understand the various modalities of the subject's appearance in works of literature. The question "Who speaks the work?" involves the analyst at least implicitly in a consideration of enunciation. And the question is as important to film as for literary studies, even though film does not use language as its sole or primary form of expression.

To understand the way the concept of enunciation has been brought into film studies one must look to Christian Metz's essay "histoire/discours," which remains the most explicit attempt to transfer Benveniste's work on enunciation to film. The essay addresses the question of the existence of a speaking subject in film, a figure comparable to the "I" in language, ostensibly the source of the film's global processes. One might be tempted to view this as just a new-fangled, "scientific" way of restating the concerns of the auteur theory, but the concept of enunciation displaces and challenges that theory's controlling myth: the notion of the director as expressive individual transcending the constraints of inherited convention. Work on enunciation would stress instead the very conventions through which the individual can accede to the position of speaking subject.

In putting forward his argument Metz has recourse to the distinction Benveniste makes between *histoire* (history or story) and *discours* (discourse). *Discours* consists of all forms of speaking and writing that assume an "I" and a "you" and that, therefore, take up the formal apparatus described earlier. *Histoire,* on the other hand, is a system restricted to written language that completely bypasses the formal apparatus of the enunciation. In *histoire* there is no reference to the enunciation or the actants involved in it. In fact, Benveniste says, "there is no longer even a narrator. The events are set forth chronologically, as they occurred. No one speaks here; the events seem to narrate themselves."[15]

Metz argues that the enunciation in film proceeds through *histoire,* not *discours.* "The very principle" of the classical film's effectiveness is that "it obliterates all traces of the enunciation, and masquerades as story."[16] Metz's proposition that film does not set out a position for the "speaking subject" is founded on a number of remarkable insights, but it finally presents a problematic, or at least narrow, picture of the classical cinema. The difficulties arise in part from the way that Metz circumscribes *histoire* as the object of his analysis. There are indeed moments in films when the narration is ungrounded, when it seems to proceed from nowhere—and Metz's thesis about the path of the spectator's identification in such instances is seminal. But there are also moments when the reception of film depends on localizing a productive instance behind the enunciation in a particular figure, whether it be the director, actor, screenwriter, or whatever. These latter moments are literally defined away in the article. Metz relegates all discursive aspects of film to the institution to define his object, the individual text (the film, the story) in opposition to it (as that which is not discursive). The text is thus constituted as a kind of ideal object that, in its positioning of the spectator, excludes all factors that could be said to be institutional (i.e., discursive) in nature.

It is the extreme formalism of Benveniste's model of enunciation that allows Metz to circumscribe the text in this way, thereby separating it from its institutional inscription. Since there is no representation of the enunciation in the enounced, Metz argues, the enunciative instance does not enter into the reception of film. This separation of the text from the institution produces an extremely reified vision of spectator-text relations. The grounds upon which the two are separated (across lines of *histoire* and *discours*) actually predetermine the effect that is then assigned to the film: that of *histoire*. But it is in many ways obvious that our relation to a film is not solely a relation to a story but also—and often consciously—a relation to the performance of that story. *Histoire* should be viewed as a specific functioning of the film text and not as the definition of its parameters.

Recent work on authorship has attempted to move beyond the formal theory of enunciation. This theory can only comprehend enunciation as a system of formal markings (available in language as a system) that manifest themselves in the linguistic syntagm. There is no recognition that the enunciation—and therefore the position of the enunciating subject—could be determined by factors external to language as a set of forms. What is specifically ignored in this theory is that enunciation takes place in a broad context of discursive practices and that one must account, at the very least, for the institutional and intertextual inscription of the speaking subject.

The application of the formal theory to film has presented some particular difficulties. In language, at least, there are formal markers that systematically trace out and represent the position of the speaking subject. Such markers (for a global subject at least) are typically absent in film; there is generally no "I" and no system of shifters or tense. The organization of the images may perhaps lead one to infer the presence of an enunciator "behind" the images, but of course it is only the traces of this presence that one encounters in the enounced. The enunciator as figure is absent.

Given this description of the enunciator in film, the formal analysis can take two tacks. It can deny that an enunciating subject ever manifests itself to the spectator and claim that the classical film functions seamlessly as *histoire*, or it can argue that the enunciating subject has a more oblique existence in film than in language, but that it nevertheless does manifest itself to the spectator. An attempt must then be made to locate the formal determinants of this manifestation.

This latter tack is obviously preferable, and the investigation it sets in motion is a productive, if limited, one. Metz himself has signaled the necessity of such an investigation by noting that an odd camera angle may break the spectator's primary identification and refer to the presence of an enunciating subject. This is characteristic of the way in which a formal analysis seizes the enunciative instance as a deviation from the norm (of *histoire*). Odd camera angles, unmotivated camera movements, moments of didacticism, ill-timed or ironic flourishes of music—all of these features that are in excess of the story tend to draw our attention to an enunciative presence. There is some validity to this approach, yet a question must be raised about the mode of existence of this enunciative presence. The formal approach would seem to suggest that this presence is self-contained in the formal markings of the film, that the enunciating subject is, in fact, merely an effect of form. Without denying the effectivity of form, I would argue that this is a problematic view.

Metz—in a move that seems to be unaccompanied by any theoretical reflection—steps outside of the methodological framework within which his other points are made to claim that the formal subject can be identified with the director. In one sense this is a welcome move: it breaks the hermeticism of the formal theory of enunciation by recognizing the enunciation's engagement of a figure exterior to the linguistic syntagm. However, in the absence of any theoretical elaboration, the status of this figure is uncertain. One could view Metz's comments simply as a return to a conventional auteurism, complete with its notion of the director as expressive individual or unifying figure. But it might be fairer, and certainly more productive, to view these comments simply as a description of the way that we as spectators deal with films. It is true that we tend to ascribe formal excesses to the activity of the director. If Metz is to be faulted it is not for mentioning this process of ascription but for naturalizing it.

It is not natural that we ascribe certain textual markings to the director or to any other agent. The paths by which we move back from the text to a figure we imagine to have produced it are forged and maintained by practices proper to the cinema as an institution. John Caughie has gone so far as to say that we, the spectators, construct this figure to account for the film's enunciation. If this is the case, one might ask from what we construct this figure. The cinema has provided the terms for this ascription, I would argue, largely through discourse that exists beyond the individual film.

And it is these terms that the present study will seek to address. The cinema has been engaged not only in the production of films but also in the production of the categories through which the production—the enunciation—of those films could be understood. The director is one such category, by many accounts the most important one. When Metz ascribes the odd camera angle to the activity of the director he is making a connection that is quite "natural" within the terms provided by the institution. The subject that manifests itself somewhat elliptically in the enounced is presented as the trace of the subject of the enunciation outside of it, as the trace of the more concrete and anthropomorphic figure of the director. Of course the naturalness of this connection depends on the assumption that the director is unproblematically the producer of the enounced text and not itself a product produced by certain rules in a certain relation to it. The task of recent work on authorship has been to challenge this assumption and attempt to describe the conditions of the director's existence in discourse.

The value of Michel Foucault's work on the author lies partially in its demonstration that the subject can be ascribed a quite specific form and function through a given institutional practice.[17] To say that a text has an author is to say much more than to say it has a subject, because the author is the product of certain practices that are not extended to most kinds of discourse. The same can be said for the actor. It is not enough to say that the actor appears as subject in film; one must go on to describe the specific conditions of its appearance in discourse, the practices that give rise to this figure and determine its function.

The emphasis Foucault places on the institutional practices that constitute the author is based on a dual critique, one whose application to the actor must now be demonstrated. First of all, the actor—like the author—cannot be viewed simply as a real individual. It is a category produced by a particular institution and given a particular function within that institution. In the next chapter I will show that "individuals" appeared in films for over ten years before the notion that they were actors began to be put forward. One could argue that these individuals were not "acting," and, in a sense, this is true. However, one must consider the fact that the very definition of what kind of activity constitutes acting is constructed through institutional practice. The distinction between acting and nonacting is not determined by the individual each time she or he appears in film. If an individual appears as an actor in a film it is not because of his or her talent or expressiveness but because of the rules that determine the individual's appearance as subject in a particular type of film practice.

Second, the actor cannot be said to exist simply at the level of film form. The actor's body does of course appear in the form of film, and thus its gestures and expressions can be seen as formal markings. Yet the bodily gestures that appear in the enounced cannot naturally be called acting nor can these gestures—from the evidence presented in the form of the film alone—be considered those of an actor. An example should clarify this point. A formally similar image of a person crying could be included in both a documentary film and a fictional film, yet the person would only be considered an actor as she or he appeared in the fiction film. It would therefore be wrong to suggest that these formal markings fully contain the actor. They are rather the traces of an identity that is constituted elsewhere, in the discourses "outside" of the film.

The body that appears in fiction films actually has an ambiguous and complex status: at any moment one can theoretically locate two bodies in the one: a body produced (that of the character) and a body producing (that of the actor). An attention to the former draws the spectator into the representation of character within the fiction. An attention to the latter, on the other hand, draws the spectator into a specific path of intertextuality that extends outside of the text as formal system. For this subject to be ascribed a productive relation to the effects registered in the enounced, it must be seen as existing in some way outside of them.

We can note a number of levels at which the actor-subject is constituted as an instance exterior to (though still clearly linked to) its appearance in form. Each is predicated on the knowledge, which the most rudimentary familiarity with the nature of the photographic apparatus assures, that the people whose image appears on film have an existence outside of that image. This knowledge applies to anyone photographed. But the actor is ascribed a quite specific mode of existence outside of the image. At the most general level, "the actor" is constituted as a profession and understood in terms of the specific function it fulfills in a particular mode of fictional production. The various techniques, preparations, and procedures that are typically employed in this task may not enter into the images, but, insofar as they enter into the broader discursive field within which the images are received, they work to define the actor. One cannot read the actor's appearance in film as such in purely formal terms. It may seem obvious, but one must first know just what kind of activity acting is, what types of discourse it appears in, its aesthetic and fictional status, etc. The actor, as the site of a particular type of work, is a category within which the image is read but is nevertheless produced—and seen as existing—outside of it.

At a more specific level the actor is individualized through the circulation of a specific image and name. One could argue that with the image, the actor's identity is very much a matter of form. But the circulation of the image actually exceeds the form of the film because the individual actor's identity is often, if not typically, constituted across a number of films. The spectator's relation to that identity in such instances is a relation to an intertextual field of associations, not merely a formal marker. These associations are organized in part through the name, which supports the actor's identity in language.

The name not only appears outside of the image, but it also refers to an identity that extends beyond the single film—into other films, into advertising preceding the film, and into other extrafilmic practices.

In fact, as the actor is increasingly individualized the name supports an expansion of the actor's identity through writing that reveals what she or he is "really like" behind the screen. The actor is assigned a personality, a love life, and perhaps even a political persuasion. As one moves back from the text to its ostensible source, one confronts a figure that is given a rather detailed, and typically "realistic," human identity.

A formal analysis would not be able to take these factors that are extrinsic to film form into account, but as I hope to demonstrate, they are very much a part of the film's enunciative apparatus. It is quite possible that in arguing for the consideration of these factors I seem to have rejected the effectivity of form. If so, let me conclude this section by clarifying my position. The close-up, the swell of music, and the facial expression obviously play an important part in the positioning of the actor as subject in film. My point is that these formal devices do not function in isolation, but rather in conjunction with categories outside of the film text, categories that the strictly formal analysis cannot account for. A broader discursive analysis is necessary if the historical and textual functioning of these categories is to be understood.

NOTES

1. Frank E. Woods, "Why Is a Star?" *Photoplay*, Nov. 1919, p. 70.

2. Ibid., p. 72.

3. Terry Ramsaye, *A Million and One Nights: A History of the Motion Picture Industry* (New York: Simon and Schuster, 1964), pp. 523–24.

4. Ibid., p. 62.

5. Benjamin Hampton, *A History of the Movies* (New York: Covici, Friede, 1931; reprinted as *History of the American Film Industry*, New York: Dover Books, 1970), p. 89.

6. Lewis Jacobs, *The Rise of the American Film: A Critical History* (New York: Harcourt, Brace, 1939), pp. 81–94.

7. Alexander Walker, *Stardom: The Hollywood Phenomenon* (New York: Stein and Day, 1970), pp. 19–39.

8. Gorham Kindem, "Hollywood's Movie Star System: A Historical Overview," in *The American Movie Industry: The Business of Moving Pictures,* ed. Gorham Kindem (Carbondale: Southern Illinois University Press, 1982), pp. 79–83.

9. Anthony Slide, "The Evolution of the Film Star," in *Aspects of American Film History Prior to 1920,* ed. Anthony Slide (Metuchen, N.J.: Scarecrow Press, 1970), pp. 1–6.

10. Hampton, *History of the American Film Industry,* p. 92.

11. Jeanne Thomas Allen, "The Decay of the Motion Picture Patents Company," in *The American Film Industry,* ed. Tino Balio (Madison: University of Wisconsin Press, 1976), pp. 119–34.

12. Janet Staiger makes a similar point in a brief section of *The Classical Hollywood Cinema.* See David Bordwell, Janet Staiger, and Kristin Thompson, *The Classical Hollywood Cinema: Film Style and Mode of Production to 1960* (New York: Columbia University Press, 1985), p. 101.

13. Roland Barthes, "La vedette, enquetes d'audience?" *Communications* 2, 1963, p. 213. My translation.

14. See Benveniste's *Problems in General Linguistics,* trans. M. E. Meek (Coral Gables: University of Miami Press, 1971), and "L'appareil formel de l'enonciation," *Langages* 17 (Mar. 1970): 12–19.

15. Benveniste, *Problems in General Linguistics,* p. 208.

16. Christian Metz, *The Imaginary Signifier,* trans. Celia Britton, Annsyl Williams, Ben Brewster, and Alfred Guzzetti (Bloomington: Indiana University Press, 1982), p. 91.

17. Michel Foucault, "What Is an Author?" in *Textual Strategies: Perspectives in Post-Structuralist Criticism,* ed. Josue V. Harari (Ithaca, N.Y.: Cornell University Press, 1979), pp. 141–60.

The Discourse on Acting

Moving pictures existed for over a decade before anything resembling a star system appeared. Although personalities from other fields (particularly politics) were presented in documentary "views" from a very early date, they were not in any strict sense of the term movie stars. The basis of their notoriety lay elsewhere. One can cite, as an example, the series of five films Edison copyrighted in 1899 documenting Admiral Dewey's role in the Spanish-American War (largely the parade upon his return). Although the cinema certainly capitalized upon Dewey's notoriety, it had neither a direct role in creating it nor the means to control it. The fame of personalities such as Dewey was caught up in a circulation of events exterior to the cinema as an institution.

The cinema's function in relation to these personalities was, in a sense, merely to represent them. Dewey, McKinley, Roosevelt, and Prince Henry were the raw material in what was principally a new form of photojournalism. This cannot be said of stars such as Florence Lawrence and Mary Pickford, who emerged out of an explicitly fictional mode of film production. The spectator did not pay to see a record of Mary Pickford's movements, but paid, rather, to see her activity in the enunciation of a fiction.

There was thus no simple continuity between the intermittent representations of these famous figures and the star as such. Nor did these representations in any clear way mark out the conditions for the emergence of the star. In fact, one cannot locate the incipience of the star system in the industry's practices prior to 1907.

Of course the question this raises is why the cinema did not have a star system before this date. The theater, vaudeville, and professional sports all banked on the ability of name performers to attract an audience. The theater had, in fact, based its popularity on star performers through much, if not most, of the nineteenth century. According to Benjamin McArthur, a theatrical star system had begun to gain momentum in America with George Frederick Cook's 1810 tour. By the 1870s, certainly, a star system dominated American theater. Star-centered combination tours were driving local stock companies out of business, and "matinee idols" such as Harry Montague (and later Kyle Bellew and Maurice Barrymore) were being hounded by hundreds of ardent female fans. In the 1880s and 1890s, Charles Frohman achieved unparalleled success as a theatrical producer by using the expanding press and the techniques of modern advertising to make stars out of Maude Adams, Ethel Barrymore, May Robson, and William Faversham. By the end of the century the theatrical star system was operating at full force.[1]

It might seem natural then that the cinema—from the beginning—would have adopted a similar strategy. But it is a mistake to assume that this presented itself as an option for the early leaders of the industry. Given the nature of the industry at the time and the early film's status as discourse, the movie star, as it would later develop, was in a very real sense unthinkable. Between 1898 and 1906 the film industry depended wholly upon such institutions as vaudeville and amusement parks as its means of exhibition. Moving pictures had a relatively restricted role in vaudeville. They were not incorporated into it as a means of mechanically reproducing the labor of star acts (so that those acts could appear in a number of theaters at once, in absentia). Although Edison's early films did present snippets of vaudeville acts and playlets, they did not catch hold in any profound way; they were soon superseded when documentary views of exterior objects and events proved more interesting. These topical genres, which dominated film production during this period, had, at best, an oblique relation to that part of the vaudeville commodity that depended upon name performers. Moving pictures were a replacement for certain vaudeville acts only in a broad, structural sense: they occupied a particular slot in the show (that which had been typically occupied by other visually oriented acts, such as pantomime spectacle, puppetry, and tableaux vivants) and fit into a tradition of entertainment that melded scientific gadgetry and visual novelty.[2] They did not replace live acts by transferring them to the screen.

Thus, owners of vaudeville houses did not see in the reproducibility of moving pictures a kind of Benjaminian solution to the increasing demand and competition for live acts. Their interest in the kinetoscope was more immediate. They saw it as a genuine novelty that, for a time at least, would attract a crowd. At first, the novelty of the cinema followed from its capacity to represent iconic movement of any kind. The kinetoscope appeared as the most sophisticated version of a long line of nineteenth-century devices, whose purpose was to do precisely this. It is not clear how long this novelty propelled interest in the cinema. Robert C. Allen argues that by 1897 "moving picture acts based their appeal less on the cinema's ability to render highly iconic representations and more on the subject matter which was represented." The system of genre that emerged and predominated film production during these years attests to this. Genres such as the documentary, travel film, newsreel, and sports film (which together accounted for 86.9 percent of production) were both characterized and differentiated by their reference to a particular field of objects and events.[3]

Still one cannot dismiss the continuing effectivity of the novelty of the technological base. The trick film (which gained popularity around 1901), although it recalled certain traditions of stage magic, depended wholly on the magical qualities of the cinematic apparatus for its effect. Even the topical film, to the extent that it represented extraordinary events, focused a good measure of attention onto the ability of the machine to "capture" them.

The question here is not whether spectators paid to see "content" or whether they paid to see the marvelous workings of the machine—they obviously paid to see both. The kinetoscope held the spectators' attention between these poles in a kind of "economy." What is important to note is that this economy precluded the kind of attention that would be the precondition for the emergence of the star—that is, an attention to the human labor involved in the production of film. Eric Smoodin has convincingly argued that early journalistic discourse of the time characterized film as a product independent of human labor.[4] What he calls a "reification of the apparatus" is clear in the titles of articles such as "Moving Pictures and the Machines Which Create Them" and "Revelations of the Camera." Such articles posited the apparatus as the singular site of textual productivity.

Thus, the enunciative position that the vaudeville performer occupied on stage was not replicated in the enunciative system of film. The activity behind a particular representation was relegated to the workings of the machine, not to the "creative" labor of humans. The kind of emphasis that would permit the emergence of the star system was impossible under these conditions.

A number of sweeping changes began to take place in the industry after 1905. The first and most important of the changes was undoubtedly the emergence of the nickelodeon as the dominant means of film exhibition. For the first time the cinema had its own exhibition outlet. This prompted a certain reorganization of the relation between production, distribution, and exhibition. As Robert C. Allen has pointed out,

> The use of films in vaudeville did not require a division of the industry into distinct production, distribution and exhibition units. In fact, it favored the collapsing of these functions into the "operator," who, with his projector, became the self-contained vaudeville act. It was not until American cinema achieved industrial autonomy with the advent of store-front movie theaters that a clear separation of functions became the dominant mode of industrial organization, and film entered its early industrial phase.[5]

One can see in the formation of the Motion Picture Patents Company in 1908 (and in fact in the earlier alliance between the Edison licensees and the Film Service Association) an attempt by the manufacturers to regularize the relations between production, distribution, and exhibition. It is, of course, no accident that this attempt at "industrial reform" was designed to form a monopoly and secure enormous profits for the producers. The Patents Trust later argued that its actions had been beneficial in that it had organized a set of chaotic practices that were hindering the expansion of the industry. And there is no doubt some truth to this.

The nickelodeon boom brought with it an exponential rise in the demand for moving pictures—a demand that the industry, as it was structured at the time, could not efficiently supply. There had been few nickelodeons prior to 1905 but by 1907 there were, by the most conservative estimates, at least 2,500. Each of these nickelodeons needed new films on a regular basis. So, a more systematic means of getting films into distribution channels and into the theaters was in order. And of course the production process itself had to be accelerated substantially. Some of the most significant changes that took place during these years stemmed from the manufacturers' attempts to meet the rising demand for films. They built more studios, set up property departments, and formed stock companies. In short, they instituted more factorylike methods to assure a regular, adequate flow of films.

Crucial to this move toward more rationalized production practices was the shift toward fictional film production. This shift began around 1902, but reached an important point of consolidation in the years 1907 and 1908. Robert C. Allen has argued that "between 1907 and 1908 a dramatic change occurred in American Motion Picture Production. In one year narrative forms of cinema (comedy and dramatic) all but eclipsed documentary forms in volume of production." Even more remarkably, the percentage of dramatic production increased from 17 to 66 percent in 1908. Allen's figures come from a consideration of copyrighted titles during those years. Charles Musser has demonstrated, by looking at the amount of footage distributed (fiction films were longer and more prints of each film were distributed), that the economics of the industry had turned toward fiction somewhat earlier, certainly by 1904.[6] But he notes the uneven development that existed between filmmaking, which "remained a cottage industry," and exhibition, "which had become a form of mass production." It is in 1907 and 1908 that film production caught up, instituting a mode of fictional filmmaking (Musser refers to it, in quotation marks, as the "'Griffith mode'") based on standardization, narrative efficiency, and maximization of profits. For Bordwell, Staiger, and Thompson, it is during these years that the primitive cinema began to give way to a mode of filmmaking that would lead to a standardized, classical style. As films lengthened, more complex narratives began to be constructed around the psychological traits of characters, and a mode of editing and shot distance emerged that stressed, beyond all else, the linearity of the narrative and the characters' goals in propelling it forward. D. W. Griffith's work at Biograph, which began in late 1908, offers the clearest and most familiar evidence of this new mode.[7]

Allen argues that this shift toward fictional production was at least in part the industry's attempt to gain control over the production situation. Prior to this shift, when topical genres dominated production, the popularity of moving pictures depended all too much upon events the industry had no control over—wars, disasters, coronations, etc. The fictional film lent itself to a more rationalized set of procedures. Production could be centralized and a rough but more efficient division of labor put in place. More important, the availability of good subjects would be a matter of imagining them, rather than finding them in the world. By focusing on fictional production the industry changed the status of film as a commodity in such a way that it could assert a greater degree of control over its defining features as a commodity. Events exterior to the cinema would no longer have such a profound and potentially devastating effect on the popularity of moving pictures. Films would be differentiated from one another by factors largely internal to, and within the control of, the cinema as an institution.

Of course, as long as the supply of films from producers was sporadic and the demand great, the problem of product differentiation fell most pointedly on the shoulders of the exhibitors. By 1907 the incredible proliferation of nickelodeons had saturated the market for moving pictures in most urban areas, causing increased competition among exhibitors for a limited number of customers. In such cases, the individual nickelodeon's success became dependent upon the extent to which it could differentiate the service it offered from that of its competitors.

Such differentiation could be effected in three ways. First of all, the physical setting of the nickelodeon could be upgraded. Exhibitors discovered that the crowded, dusty storefront (the stereotypical nickelodeon) could not compete with more comfortable, opulent moving picture theaters. The latter were not only more attractive to regular nickelodeon customers, but they also drew in a more upscale audience that perhaps enjoyed moving pictures in vaudeville but (because of class divisions) had been left out of the initial nickelodeon boom.[8]

Second, vaudeville acts could be introduced back into moving picture presentations. This happened increasingly after 1907 and culminated in small-time vaudeville, which interspersed film and vaudeville acts in larger capacity theaters. The theater was one aspect of this scheme, but exhibitors could also attract customers with the quality of their live acts.

Finally, exhibitors could attempt to offer either more frequent program changes or better films than their competitors. Unfortunately, this strategy involved factors over which the exhibitor typically had very little control. A regular flow of films was often very difficult to come by. Furthermore, the manufacturers were not putting out a product that was designed to give the exhibitor leverage in this increasingly competitive situation. This is not to say that all of the films were bad or that all were the same. The point is that the shift toward fictional film production did not automatically bring with it a system of product differentiation commensurate with the needs of the exhibitors.

It should be noted that the labor involved in moving pictures—to the extent that it was emphasized—appeared at the level of exhibition. In the early days of the cinematograph the moving picture "act" consisted not only of the film but of the projectionist as well, and lecturers often accompanied films with commentary throughout this period. Thus, a live entertainer, much in the tradition of vaudeville, held an intermediary position between the audience and the film. With the star system, we see a shift of attention away from this performance at the level of exhibition and toward the labor that began to manifest itself at the level of production—that is, the performance of those who appeared in films.

It is in this context that one must view the earliest appearance of the discourse on acting. Around 1907 a number of articles began to appear that placed into the foreground the role of human labor in the production of film. This should not be viewed as a demystification of the means of production but rather as the regulated appearance of a certain kind of knowledge. This knowledge entered into a struggle destined to resituate the site of textual productivity for the spectator away from the work of the apparatus itself. A number of potential "sites of productivity" were involved in this struggle—the manufacturer, the cinematographer (or director), and the photoplaywright, but of course it was the actor/star that finally became central in this regard.

In May of 1907 a series of articles began to appear in *Moving Picture World* entitled "How the Cinematographer Works and Some of His Difficulties." These articles offered a general account of the labor involved in producing films and focused a large measure of attention on the labor of those who appeared in films. The first installment began,

> Should you ever seek the source of the moving pictures of the vaudeville theater, you will learn that the comic, the tragic, the fantastic, the mystic scenes so swiftly enacted in photographic pantomime are not real but feigned. You will find that the kinetoscopic world is much like the dramatic, that it has its actors and actresses, its playwrights and stage directors, its theatrical machinery, its wings, its properties, its lights, its tricks, its make-ups, its costumes, its entrances and its exits.[9]

In exposing the creative labor at the "source" of the moving picture, the article makes a direct appeal to a theatrical model. The reader is told that those who appear on screen are actors and is to assume, it seems, that their activity is acting. This, however, becomes somewhat problematic if we believe the definition of the "picture performer" given in the next installment of the series:

> Those who make a business out of posing for the kinetoscope are called 'picture performers' and many a hard knock they have to take. Practically all of them are professional stage people, and while performing on Broadway at night they pick up a few dollars day times in a moving picture studio. In a variety show, therefore, it sometimes happens that the same tumblers who a moment ago were turning handsprings and somersaults in real life, again appear in such roles as the traditional "Rube" and the "green goods man," but only in a phantom form upon the pictured screen.[10]

We can see something of a retreat from a theatrical model in this passage. Although the article claims that the performers are professional stage people, the example that follows seems to indicate that their stage is that of vaudeville, not theater. Acting is not mentioned here. Those who occupy the "traditional roles" are not actors, but tumblers.

It is not difficult to understand why the labor involved in the production of film would be symbolized through a comparison with the vaudeville act. The moving picture industry retained strong institutional ties to vaudeville, even though the nickelodeon was strongly challenging vaudeville as the dominant outlet of exhibition. As the quotation indicates, moving pictures had typically appeared alongside live vaudeville acts. It seems quite logical that the activity of the "picture performer" would, from the start, be set within the tradition of performance that characterized vaudeville.

However, it was a discourse on acting and therefore a theatrical model that would, over the next couple of years, define and determine the enunciative status of those who appeared in films. The above passage demonstrates, among other things, the equivocation with which this discourse was put forward. One notes a certain tentativeness in the symbolization of the performer's labor in terms of acting in much of the writing of the period. Acting was a profession associated with the legitimate stage, and the contention that people acted in films was neither immediately apparent nor altogether un-problematic. As we shall see later, the "film actor" emerged in a particularly contradictory field of discourses and traditions of enter-tainment.

"How the Cinematographer Works and Some of His Difficulties" appeared as an initiatory attempt to define and situate the work of those involved in the production of moving pictures. In particular, these articles (and others like them that began to appear in the last half of 1907) worked to constitute the "picture performer" or "film actor" as a subject of discourse. In so doing, they precipitated a significant shift in the enunciative status of film. Much of the knowl-edge that emerged about the picture performer in these early articles proceeded through a highly conventionalized form of narrative. The same type of stories appear again and again in explanations of the performer's work. All of the stories were predicated on the distinc-tion drawn in the previous passage between the "phantom form on the screen" and the real performer and, more generally, between the filmic and profilmic.[11] The real performer's role in the profilmic event was the subject of all of these stories.

Note, for instance, this description of the filming of a bank robbery scene:

> In the most realistic way, the "robbers" broke into the bank, held up the cashier, shot a guard "dead" who attempted to come to the rescue, grabbed up a large bundle of money, and made their escape. Thus far all went well. The thieves were running down the street with the police in pursuit, just as the picture had been planned, when an undertaker, aroused by the racket, looked out of his shop. One glance sufficed to tell him that the time had come at last when he might become a hero. The "robbers" were heading toward him, and, leaping into the middle of the sidewalk, he aimed a revolver at the foremost fugitive with the threat: "Stop, thief, or I'll blow your brains out."[12]

The undertaker apprehended both of the bandits and refused to release them until he was convinced, by the head of the bank, that the robbery was staged.

Another story is prefaced by the following claim: "It may sometimes be said that the picture performer becomes so engrossed in his work that he forgets that he is simply shamming.[13] What follows is a story about the filming of a scene in which the hero must rescue a drowning girl. A crowd of bystanders who thought the girl was really drowning jumped into the lake to rescue her. The hero seemed to forget it was all an act, and—not to be outdone by his competition—raced to rescue the girl.

Both of these stories play upon a confusion between the filmic, the profilmic, and the real, but they do so primarily as a way of making distinctions between the three. The possibility of these distinctions was a necessary condition for the emergence of the picture performer. First of all, this emergence depended upon a knowledge of the performer's existence outside of the narrative of the film itself. By introducing the contingency of the profilmic event into what is otherwise a simple retelling of the (planned) narrative of the film, these stories differentiate the profilmic from the filmic and ascribe the former a relatively distinct status. Another narrative is set forth (separable from that of the film) that takes as its subject the performer's part in the production of film. These stories not only distinguish the profilmic from the filmic, they also, more obviously perhaps, distinguish the profilmic from the real. In straightening the two out the performer—and the reader—must confront the fictional status of that which is photographed by the camera.

The attention to the fictiveness of the scenes enacted in moving pictures had a direct bearing on the status of those who appeared in films, because it worked to establish the filmed body as a site of fictional production. It would be wrong to suggest that the body had not supported fictional material prior to 1907 because much evidence exists to the contrary. However, many of the early articles that described the work of those who appeared in films (such as "How the Cinematographer Works and Some of His Difficulties") were clearly under the sway of—or at least struggling with—a quite different, more established conception of the filmed body.

This conception was rooted in a photographic tradition and is manifested most clearly in the use of the verb *pose* in many of these early articles. In photography the pose is, in a sense, the limit of the body's complicity with the act of representation. The photograph may be posed or unposed, but it is not, within dominant practice at least, anything else. The verb *pose* may have described fairly unproblematically the nature of the activity of those who were represented in the topical, "documentary" films that dominated production prior to 1907. But it did not adequately account for the activity of those who appeared in dramatic or comedic films, because the pose does not usually carry connotations of a fictional production. The posed body is admittedly a highly conventionalized one; as Barthes has noted, in posing one transforms oneself in advance into an image.[14] Yet it is only in the context of the tension between the conventionality of the pose and the existence of a more spontaneous bodily identity that the "truth" of the pose is typically called into question. The more fundamental belief that the photograph represents something real remains undisputed. The fact that a picture is posed does not therefore necessarily lead to the conclusion that it is less real, that it is fictional or faked.

The shift in the status of the filmed body after 1907 was built precisely on this conclusion, however. Although the photographic conception of the body retained a kind of currency, it could not unproblematically accommodate the activity of those who were engaged in the presentation of a fiction. From 1907 we can see a kind of struggle between a photographic conception of the body and a theatrical one—between posing and acting. The ascendancy of the latter followed in part because it could account for the body as the site of a fictional production.

A correlation obviously exists between the consolidation of fictional filmmaking in 1907 and 1908 and the emergence of the discourse on acting. How is this correlation to be understood? Was the discourse on acting caused by this shift in production or vice versa?

One must guard against these overly simple views to stress the complexity of the interaction between these two levels.

The fictional film existed long before the notion that people acted in films. As we have seen, the discourse on acting only appeared at the point at which the fiction film became the dominant, standardized product of the manufacturers. I have argued that the increasing dominance of the fictional film rendered the photographic conception of the body ("posing," "modeling") problematic and called for a model that could account for the body as a site of a fictional production. The theatrical model—and "acting"—met this requirement (as did other designations such as "faking" and, more ambiguously, "performing"). Insofar as it did, the discourse on acting can be seen as a response to the shift in film production. However, it would be a mistake to assume that the discourse on acting was simply a descriptive response. Although "acting" could account for the fictional status of the filmed body, in other respects it was an inappropriate description of the activity of those who appeared in films between 1907 and 1909. The moving pictures of the time generally provided little evidence to support acting's associations with art, expression, and interiority.

In fact, much writing of this period implicitly called into question the descriptive capacity of the discourse on acting: "the repertoire actor has discovered a new use for his talents. He is now a moving picture. That is, he now poses for moving pictures. By lying down, rolling over and jumping in front of the camera he is able to earn in three days a sum equal to a week's salary at his former industry."[15] Although the writer acknowledges that actors appear in films he must, for obvious reasons, stop short of claiming that their activity is acting. "Lying down, rolling over and jumping" are not what one thinks of when one thinks of an acting performance. Yet it was this kind of broad action (however parodically it is portrayed here) that characterized most of the films of the day.

For this reason, writers often made the claim that people acted in films with a marked degree of irony or irresolution. The word *actor* (and *artist*), for instance, usually appeared in quotation marks in these early articles. Note the following description of the making of a fiction film: "A man skilled at the business will impersonate the miserable husband in the case and a vaudeville actress temporarily out of work will play the role of the wife. Having secured permission of the city authorities to have a lot of sham disorder in the streets, the head man sends out photographers and 'actors.'"[16] The quotation marks allow the writer to assert that actors appear in films while acknowledging the problematic status of that assertion—and in fact making a joke out of it.

A similar tack is taken by Walter Prichard Eaton in "The Canned Drama." Eaton begins by describing an encounter with a professional actor friend who had turned to moving picture work. Yet, later in the article, Eaton parodies the contention that professional actors appear in films by distinguishing between two horses on a movie set. The horse that had cooperated with the director was apparently a professional actor while the more recalcitrant one was "merely an amateur."[17]

The tentative, contradictory treatment that film acting received in much of this early writing was prompted by the disjunction between the aesthetic pretensions of the discourse on acting and the types of films being produced at the time. It should be clear that the discourse on acting did not emerge simply because people acted in films. There was obviously some uncertainty about *what* people did in moving pictures. The discourse on acting worked against rather contradictory evidence to assert and establish the "fact" that people acted in films. It therefore had an active role in the changes taking place in the production and reception of moving pictures; it was not merely an effect or a reflection of those changes.

In fact, it was not until well after the discourse on acting emerged that films began to appear that fully supported and gave credence to the claim that people acted in films. The most famous and influential of these films were the French Films D'Art distributed by the Pathé Company. The films were offered by reviewers as proof that the art of acting could be translated to the screen:

The greatest improvement at present (and there is still plenty of room for more) is along the line of dramatic structure and significant acting. Does it sound silly to talk thus pedantically, in the language of dramatic criticism, about moving pictures? If you will watch a poor American picture unroll blinkingly, and then a good French one, you will feel that it is not silly after all.

With reference to the Pathé Film D'Art, "The Return of Ulysses," to which I referred last week, it is interesting to point out that the story was written by Jules Lemaitre, of the Academie Francaise, and the principal characters are taken by Mme. Bartet, MM. Albert Lambert, Lelauny and Paul Mounet, all of the Comedie Francaise, Paris. This is equivalent to David Belasco and his Stuyvesant company doing the work for the Edison Company. Again I say, American Manufacturers please note![18]

The artistic pretensions of the discourse on acting were clearly borne out by these films. The Films D'Art were a series of films produced in a Neuilly studio by a production group of the same name and controlled and distributed by Pathé. Although the group began making films in 1908 their early efforts were not released in the United States until 1909. A certain amount of American publicity accompanied their production, however, and therefore preceded their release here. A French correspondent for *Variety*, reporting in July 1908, announced that some of France's greatest playwrights were "writing versions of the best works for famous actors to play—before the camera." As an example he noted that Hugenot, "the latest member of our great national stage," was appearing before the camera in *Blanchette* under the direction of Germier. Elsewhere it was rumored that Bernhardt, Duse, and "other great actresses of the day" were performing their greatest theatrical successes on film for Pathé.[19]

The first Film D'Art released in America, in February 1909, was entitled *Incriminating Evidence*. The *New York Dramatic Mirror* reacted to it this way: "It promises to be the most important dramatic subject ever issued by any company. It is acted by Severin, the great French pantomimist, who has proven one of the vaudeville sensations of the year in America. He is assisted in the film by his own company." The second American release (which had actually been the first produced) was *The Assassination of the Duke de Guise*. The names of the famous actors who appeared in the films were given a great deal of prominence in reviews and publicity, as they had been for the Severin picture: "The story was written for Pathe Freres by M. Henri Levedan of the Academie Francaise, and the chief parts were played by Mlle. Robinne and Mssrs. Lebargy and Albert Lambert of the Comedie Francaise." The *Dramatic Mirror* immediately hailed the film as "one of the few masterpieces of motion picture production."[20]

The Film D'Art series continued, apparently in monthly releases, with such films as *The Tower of Nesle* from the novel by Dumas (September 1909), *Drink* from *L'Assomoir* by Zola (October 1909), *Rigoletto* from Verdi's opera (November 1909), and *La Grande Breteche* from the novel by Balzac (December 1909).[21] The publicity surrounding the first three of these films did not call any special attention to specific actors. It made more general claims about the artfulness of these films. For instance, we are told that *The Tower of Nesle* is "enacted by the leading exponents of dramatic art," and that *Drink* is the "greatest picture ever produced." The ads that appeared for *La Grande Breteche* made similar claims, but they also stressed the cast—Phillipe Garnier of the Comédie Française, André Calamettes of the Gymanase, and Mlle. Sergine of L'Odéon.[22]

It should be noted that Pathé released other prestige pictures during this time which were not technically part of the Film D'Art series. *Her Dramatic Career*, for instance, received the same kind of publicity as *La Grande Breteche*, a month before the latter's release. And one reviewer judged an earlier effort, *The Hand* (from February of 1909), to be in the same class as the initial Films D'Art.[23] The Films D'Art were the most visible examples of a more general interest Pathé had in "high-class" productions.

Early Film D'Art releases of 1910 presented Mlle. Victoria Lepanto in *Carmen* and *The Lady with the Camelias*. Although Lepanto received more publicity than any actor who had previously appeared in Films D'Art, nothing was said to imply that she had a theatrical background. This marks a significant departure from earlier practice and takes us into the province of the picture personality. The Film D'Art's supreme contribution to the contention that people acted in films probably did not come until 1912 with the release of a filmed version of *Camille* starring Sarah Bernhardt. Bernhardt's entry into moving pictures had been long awaited. Her capitulation was seen as "a milestone in the evolution of the moving picture."[24] The world's greatest and most famous actress (by many accounts at least) had become a photoplayer, thus blurring—for an instant at least—all distinctions between the moving picture and the legitimate theater.

Camille was not different from the initial efforts of the Film D'Art in kind so much as degree. Bernhardt's name was a household word while those of Robinne and Lebargy were not. "Bernhardt" had attained the status of a popular symbol, the name itself signifying the art of great acting. The producers certainly took this into account when they paid Bernhardt a reported $30,000 to appear before the camera. The promoters of *Camille* (as well as those who promoted *Queen Elizabeth*, Bernhardt's next film) capitalized on it with an intensive publicity campaign, and the many journalists who had an interest in advancing the aesthetic legitimacy of the cinema used it to make some of their most zealous claims. *Camille* apparently succeeded. According to the publicity for the film and an attendant article in *Moving Picture News* the film was the "fastest seller ever offered States Rights buyers."[25]

The theatrical model, which had been taken up somewhat awkwardly by the discourse on acting in discussions of other films, was fully embodied by the Film D'Art. The comparisons between the theater and moving pictures were quite appropriate here. The Films D'Art, after all, were moving pictures of theatrical plays. Because of this, it probably seemed natural (as well as expedient) to emphasize the performance of the actors involved and publicize their names. Plays were promoted and consumed in this way. The enunciative position that the theatrical actor assumed in the theater was reproduced in these films. The notion of the film actor emerged through its association with this established tradition.

The Films D'Art have a prominent place in this history not because they were the first films of their kind (though this is arguable), but because they were the most visible, the most regularly released, and the most influential. Writers quite commonly held the films up to the public and to the American producers as the foremost examples of film art. For many they represented the future of the moving picture industry—that ideal point at which the theater and the cinema would seamlessly merge to elevate the tastes of the masses to an appreciation of theatrical art. This future was not realized of course; the cinema would not become "filmed theater." Nevertheless, the Film D'Art had a significant impact on the course the cinema took during these years.

Developments in American production paralleled the "advances" of the Film D'Art. Manufacturers began to release prestige pictures—adaptations of famous literary and dramatic works—as early as 1907. Kalem released a version of *Ben Hur* in late 1907 that later became famous in connection with a copyright decision regarding adaptations. By March of 1908 Selig had produced versions of *The Count of Monte Cristo, Dr. Jekyll and Mr. Hyde,* and *Rip Van Winkle,* and Vitagraph released *The Story of Treasure Island* and *Francesca da Rimini.* Vitagraph, in fact, was the company that most vigorously pursued a policy of producing "artful" adaptations on a regular basis. At least five adaptations of plays by Shakespeare were produced by Vitagraph in 1908.[26] The manufacturers in presenting these adaptations attempted to both exploit the already constituted fame of these titles and establish the aesthetic legitimacy of moving pictures. The films worked toward this latter end by taking up a theatrical model and giving support to the discourse on acting. One does not, after all, "pose" the role of Macbeth. The very existence of some of these films gave credence to the contention that people acted in films.

Reviews of these films often noted the acting and discussed its quality. "The leading role and character part executed by the man who plays the double life of Dr. Jekyll—at times Mr. Hyde—is so convincing that no greater display of ability to fulfill this role could be shown by any actor. . . . Throughout the performance the scenes are as realistic as in any theater." "The acting of the principal characters in Richard III is all that can be desired, the only blemish being in the battle where the smiles on the faces of the actors are ill-timed."[27] One expects such references to acting in reviews today, but they were exceptional at the time.

Vitagraph's activities in prestige production accelerated in 1909. In February, a version of *Virginius* appeared that was "said to be" (by the promoters no doubt) "another step higher in the excellent work of the Vitagraph players." Ads for the film stressed that it was "elaborately staged, gorgeously costumed, superbly acted." This became the slogan for Vitagraph's prestige pictures, which soon appeared under the designation "High Art" films. Another name, *Film de Luxe,* was given to a number of films (among them a series of five films derived from Hugo's *Les Misérables*).[28] These designations clearly associated Vitagraph's quality productions with the type of film bearing the name *Film D'Art.*

There was, however, at least one significant difference between a Film D'Art such as *Incriminating Evidence* (released in February 1909) and the Vitagraph films (such as *Virginius*) released around the same time. The latter did not exploit the names of actors. We do not see an effort on the part of American producers to adopt this strategy until the middle of 1909. Vitagraph's move in this direction came in May, with a High Art production of *Oliver Twist.* An ad in the *New York Dramatic Mirror* announced that Miss Elita Proctor Otis appeared in the film "as Nancy Sykes, the role which this eminent actress has made famous throughout the world."[29] The ad displayed Otis's name prominently, in bold-face type the same size as that used for the title.

This did not, by any means, become standard practice for Vitagraph. In fact, most of the High Art films that followed *Oliver Twist* were not marketed in this way (though there was a continued emphasis on the superb acting in the films). One can argue that this was because truly famous actors were not appearing in the films. Yet the company claimed that they were, and—without naming names—they continued to use this as a selling point:

Several notable productions of the Shakespeare drama have been made by the Vitagraph and these have excited unstinted praise from the dramatic commentators, but *The Twelfth Night* is to be the best of all and the most elaborate preparations are being made. . . . A Shakespearean player of country-wide fame is one of the Vitagraph producers, and he has been given absolutely a free hand in the selection of special players. If the Vitagraph could announce the cast of characters on the sheet you would be astonished at the display of familiar names.[30]

Although the Edison Company had produced adaptations previously (a 1903 version of *Uncle Tom's Cabin,* for instance) they do not seem to have had a strong role in the high-class-film movement until the latter half of 1909, when they produced a version of *The Prince and the Pauper* with Miss Cecil Spooner:

Miss Cecil Spooner was especially employed to enact the difficult role of Tom Canty, the pauper boy, and Edward, the boy prince of Wales in Mark Twain's celebrated story, *The Prince and the Pauper.* Graceful, effective and polished as an actress, her finished art has contributed much to the beauty and strength of this notable silent drama.

We hope to employ others as well-known [as Spooner] in the near future and meantime we are building up our own force with care and discrimination.

We intend from time to time (as we have in the past) to put out especially high class pictures, based on familiar themes or plots of well-known playwrights and literary producers, with actors of known reputation. And these special pictures, sold as they will be at the same price will, we believe, commend themselves strongly to the trade as an indication of what the Edison Company is willing to do to advance the interests of the business.[31]

The earlier high-class films mentioned here may have been produced, but they were not accompanied by a comparable amount of publicity. And they certainly were not part of a regular policy of manufacturing and promoting films with well-known actors.

In September 1909, *Moving Picture World* published a cast list of the Edison film *Ethel's Luncheon*. None of the cast members were famous. The list itself served to stress the "fact" that the film contained actors, and that it should be received much as a play would be received. But the Edison Company's great coup was the engagement of the French pantomimist Pilar-Morin in September of 1909. Pilar-Morin was known in America, having toured successfully as a special attraction in Vaudeville. Her first film with the Edison Company was *Comedy and Tragedy*. An article in the *Edison Kinetogram* (later reproduced in *Moving Picture World*) authored by Pilar-Morin and entitled "The Value of Silent Drama; or Pantomime in Acting" accompanied its release.[32] In it, Pilar-Morin argues that the art of pantomime is at the base of all great drama, thus effacing the differences not only between pantomime and legitimate theater, but also between pantomime (itself a respected cultural form) and moving pictures. She ends by praising the great advances of the Edison Company in "elevating the art of moving pictures" and in "securing well-known artists and actors."

There is every reason to believe that Cecil Spooner and Elita Proctor Otis's appearances in film were, at the time, designed as one-shot ventures. Edison obviously engaged Pilar-Morin on a more long-term basis. Although she only appeared in special releases, she became in effect the star member of the Edison stock company. After *Comedy and Tragedy* she appeared in at least six other films: *The Japanese Peach Boy*, *Carmen*, *The Cigarette Maker of Seville*, *The Piece of Lace*, *From Tyranny to Liberty*, and *The Key of Life*.

These films were released at the time picture personalities were beginning to achieve fame for their work in moving pictures. Pilar-Morin has a transitional and somewhat ambiguous status in this history. On the one hand she clearly fits into the tradition of Severin and Proctor—actors whose appearance in moving pictures traded upon their fame as actors outside of moving pictures. It is in this sense that she was such a central figure in articulating the discourse on acting. However, on the other hand, she was promoted through an intense publicity campaign that not only pointed to the fact that an accomplished actor was appearing in films, but also attempted to establish her identity across a number of films as something that was marketable. She became a personality:

> Mlle. Pilar-Morin has come at the psychological moment, or, it may also be put, she is a happy accident—very gifted, very optimistic and very earnest. Curiosity as to the personalities of leading artists connected with the opera and the stage is becoming duplicated in the moving picture field, where, in the last few months, the renowned and the favorite performers have become familiar to the 7,000,000 public of the United States. The most renowned of them all, who easily takes pride of place in virtue of her record and her transcendental ability is Mme. Pilar-Morin.[33]

Later in this article Pilar-Morin's notion that the silent drama is "the expression of one's personality in one's acting" is voiced. As we shall see in the next chapter it is this notion that characterized the kind of knowledge that emerged to create the picture personality. It can be argued, in fact, that throughout 1910 Pilar-Morin functioned for the Edison Company in much the same way (though probably not as successfully) as Florence Lawrence and Florence Turner did for Imp and Vitagraph. The notable difference is that Lawrence and Turner never had any previous fame as actors outside of moving pictures.

The Biograph Company's activities during this time should be noted. Biograph did produce a number of theatrical and literary adaptations between 1907 and 1910.[34] It did not, however, publicize the names of its actors, whether famous or not. In this respect, it can be said that Biograph refrained from participating fully in the strategy pursued by Vitagraph and Edison. Yet the Biograph films did strongly emphasize acting and did therefore support the discourse on acting, even if it did so with somewhat less fanfare. A review of *The Better Way* in August 1909 stated that the film's "good acting is the point."[35] And, as we shall see in a moment, *The Better Way* was later held up as an example of a film with pure acting. Even as early as May 1909 the *New York Dramatic Mirror* could claim:

> The progress that is being made by American film manufacturers along the lines of higher dramatic art in picture pantomime is probably best illustrated by the results that have been accomplished by the Biograph Company. It is no reflection on the other American manufacturers and the great improvement they are all making to assert that the Biograph Company at present is producing a better general average of dramatic pantomime than any other company in America. If we except Pathe Freres, this claim for the Biograph may be extended to include the world.[36]

The rising emphasis on a theatrical model of "fine acting" during this period culminated in the formation of the Famous Players Film Company in 1912. Adolph Zukor set up the company specifically with the intent of presenting great theatrical actors in prestigious roles. The company would be more exclusively identified with this kind of prestige production than the other American companies, which only produced them intermittently. Zukor entered into an agreement with Daniel Frohman, a respected manager of theatrical actors, and Charles Frohman, a powerful producer on Broadway, to assure a steady stream of talent and material and, no doubt, to give his venture the stamp of respectability. Although Mary Pickford soon became Famous Players's biggest star (of course by this time she could be billed as a great actress, having conquered Broadway), and the company's reliance on the theater eventually weakened, during its early years it presented such renowned legitimate actors as Sarah Bernhardt, Mrs. Fiske, Jack Barrymore, and James K. Hackett.[37] These efforts further supported the idea that actors appeared in films and in fact exploited the public's desire to see identifiable figures acting on the screen.

As noted earlier, though, this desire was not a natural one; it had a specific history and had in fact been solicited in the years following 1907. Previous histories of the star system have largely ignored the appearance and elaboration of the discourse on acting. This chapter has traced the early history of this discourse and argued that it was through this discourse that the idea of the film actor was constituted. Around 1907 attention began to be focused away from the projectionist and the mechanical capabilities of the apparatus and toward the human labor involved in the production of film. Specifically, attention was turned to those who appeared in films, and their activity began to be characterized, after a theatrical model, as acting. In effect, a system of enunciation was put in place that featured the actor as subject. This institutionalized a mode of reception in which the spectator regarded the actor as the primary source of aesthetic effect. It is the identity of the actor as subject that would be elaborated as the star system developed.

It is clear that the symbolic work that established the actor as subject is closely linked to a specific economic strategy. The status of film as enunciation clearly changed through the discourse on acting; but it can also be said that the actor changed the status of film as commodity. The discourse on acting emerged at a time of a rapid expansion of the film industry. Companies were faced with the need to rationalize production and produce a larger and more predictable supply of films. The move toward fictional production and the formation of stock companies can be seen as a response to this need. The companies were faced with another problem within this environment—how to differentiate any of their films from the hundreds of other films on the market. Their company name and the genre of the particular film accomplished this to a degree, but not to the degree or with the force that the presence of an actor would. Films with actors could be differentiated from films without actors, and, as the presence of actors became accepted as the norm, particular actors (their identities) could be differentiated from other actors. Product differentiation quite typically follows a semiotic scheme in which differences in meaning become differences in value in an economic exchange. The discourse on acting began to put in place a system of product differentiation that would be based on the identity of the subject within an institutionalized system of enunciation.

1. See Benjamin McArthur, *Actors and American Culture, 1880–1920* (Philadelphia: Temple University Press, 1984), and David Carroll, *The Matinee Idols* (London: Peter Owen, 1972).

2. See Robert C. Allen, *Vaudeville and Film 1895–1915: A Study in Media Interaction* (New York: Arno Press, 1980). My discussion of the industry prior to 1907 owes a great deal to Allen's analysis.

3. Ibid., pp. 127, 128.

4. Eric Smoodin, "Attitudes of the American Printed Medium toward the Cinema: 1894–1908," unpublished paper, University of California, Los Angeles, 1979.

5. Allen, p. 105.

6. Ibid., pp. 212, 213; Charles Musser, "Another Look at the 'Chaser Theory,'" *Studies in Visual Communication* 10, no. 4 (Fall 1984): 24–44.

7. Charles Musser, "The Nickelodeon Era Begins: Establishing the Framework for Hollywood's Mode of Representation," *Framework* 22–23 (Autumn 1983): 4; David Bordwell, Janet Staiger, and Kristin Thompson, *The Classical Hollywood Cinema: Film Style and Mode of Production to 1960* (New York: Columbia University Press, 1985); On Griffith and Biograph see Tom Gunning's important work, *D. W. Griffith and the Origins of American Narrative Film: The Early Years at Biograph* (Urbana: University of Illinois Press, 1991).

8. See Allen, *Vaudeville and Film 1895–1915*, pp. 192–260.

9. "How the Cinematographer Works and Some of His Difficulties," *Moving Picture World*, May 18, 1907, p. 165.

10. Ibid., June 8, 1907, p. 212.

11. The events and actions that appear on screen are, in terms of this distinction, filmic. The profilmic designates the existence of those events (whether staged or unstaged) in real time and space before the camera. See Etienne Souriau, *L'univers filmique* (Paris: Flammarion, 1953).

12. "How the Cinematographer Works," *Moving Picture World*, May 18, 1907, p. 166.

13. Ibid., June 8, 1907, p. 21.

14. Roland Barthes, *Camera Lucida*, trans. Richard Howard (New York: Hill and Wang, 1981), pp. 10–15.

15. *Moving Picture World*, Oct. 21, 1907, p. 453.

16. Ibid., Aug. 29, 1908, p. 94.

17. Walter Prichard Eaton, "The Canned Drama," *American Magazine* 68 (Sept. 1909), pp. 493–500.

18. Ibid., p. 499; *Moving Picture World*, Mar. 20, 1909, p. 326.

19. *Variety*, July 7, 1908, p. 11; *Moving Picture World*, Sept. 5, 1908, p. 177.

20. *New York Dramatic Mirror*, Feb. 27, 1909, pp. 18, 13.

21. *Moving Picture World*, Sept. 25, 1909, p. 426; Oct. 23, 1909, p. 557; Nov. 13, 1909, p. 671; Dec. 4, 1909, p. 789.

22. Ibid., Oct. 23, 1909, p. 557; Dec. 4, 1909, p. 789.

23. Ibid., Nov. 13, 1909, p. 671; *New York Dramatic Mirror*, Feb. 27, 1909, p. 13.

24. *Moving Picture World*, Feb. 26, 1910, p. 294; Feb. 17, 1912, p. 596; see also *New York Times*, Sept. 15, 1911, p. 9.

25. The figure of $30,000 was of course part of the publicity and, as with all such figures, must be taken with a degree of suspicion; *Moving Picture News*, Mar. 16, 1912, p. 1089; see also *Moving Picture World*, Mar. 9, 1912, p. 874.

26. *Moving Picture World*, Feb. 1, 1908, p. 70; Mar. 7, 1908, p. 194; May 2, 1908, p. 406; Mar. 7, 1908, p. 195; Feb. 8, 1908, p. 103; Apr. 25, 1908, p. 374; Oct. 3, 1908, p. 25; Jan. 2, 1909, p. 21. For a broader account of the issues raised by the Vitagraph "quality" films, see Roberta Pearson and William Uricchio's forthcoming book, *Invisible Viewers, Inaudible Voices: Intertextuality and Reception in the Early Cinema* (Princeton, N.J.: Princeton University Press).

27. *Moving Picture World*, Mar. 7, 1908, p. 194; Oct. 3, 1908, p. 253.

28. *New York Dramatic Mirror*, Feb. 6, 1909, p. 19, 18; see, for instance, *Moving Picture World*, June 19, 1909, p. 862, and July 17, 1909, p. 79; Aug. 7, 1909, p. 184.

29. *New York Dramatic Mirror*, May 1, 1909, p. 43.

30. *Moving Picture World*, Aug. 14, 1909, p. 64.

31. *The Edison Kinetogram*, Aug. 1, 1909, p. 14, and *Moving Picture World*, Aug. 28, 1909, p. 277.

32. *The Edison Kinetogram*, Sept. 15, 1909, p. 3; Nov. 15, 1909, pp. 12–13; *Moving Picture World*, Nov. 13, 1909, p. 682.

33. *Moving Picture World*, Jan. 22, 1910, p. 204.

34. See Tom Gunning, "D. W. Griffith and the Narrator-System: Narrative Structure and Industry Organization in Biograph Films, 1908–1909" (Ph.D. diss., New York University, 1986), pp. 342–50.

35. *Moving Picture World*, Aug. 21, 1909, p. 253.

36. *New York Dramatic Mirror*, May 1, 1909, p. 34.

37. *Moving Picture World*, Jan. 11, 1913, p. 123; Aug. 23, 1913, pp. 854–55; July 11, 1914, p. 186; *Moving Picture News*, Aug. 2, 1913, p. 12; Jan. 17, 1914, p. 34.

The Picture Personality

THE discourse on acting set the conditions for the emergence of the star system. By 1909 the filmed body had been established as a site of textual productivity, as subject in an enunciative process; this enunciative process had been symbolized in terms of an aesthetics of acting, thus establishing its fictional status and lending it an air of artistic legitimacy; and, finally, the actor, thus constituted, had entered into and shifted the status of film as a commodity; it had been recognized as a viable means of product differentiation, as something that could be exploited and advertised to increase business for a particular film.

One might argue that these three factors define the movie star as such and that the appearance of such actors as Severin, Spooner, and Pilar-Morin thus marked the beginning of the star system. But there is an important distinction to be made between the legitimate actors that made appearances in film after 1907 and picture personalities such as Florence Lawrence, Florence Turner, Marion Leonard, F. X. Bushman, and King Baggot, who began to become famous in 1909 and 1910.

First, and most important, a different kind of intertextuality supported the two. In reading a film with Cecil Spooner in it, for instance, and in constructing her identity, the spectator navigated an intertextual path that moved back from the film directly to a discourse produced by the institution of the theater. A picture personality such as Florence Lawrence, in contrast, might have been said to be a fine actor, and her theatrical background might have been noted, but her identity was not based primarily on her past theatrical affiliation. It was instead constructed through the films she had appeared in and the publicity for those films. Thus, the intertextuality that constituted the identity of the picture personality was produced and maintained largely by the cinema itself; it did not depend so much on outside reference. In a sense this kind of intertextuality empowered the spectator. Most people could not claim to have seen Spooner in any other roles, and thus her reputation was a matter of received knowledge, not something the spectator could feel actively involved in judging. With the picture personality the spectator was encouraged to follow through all of the associations created through a specific actor's appearance from film to film. The more films the spectator saw, and the more she or he focused on the actors, the richer the associations would be. The fame of the picture personality was something the audience could feel it was actively participating in. It was not a matter of accepting a preestablished canon.

Of course, for the intertextual meaning that created the picture personality to arise, the individual actor had to appear quite regularly in films. This regularity is another important difference between the legitimate actors that appeared in films and the picture personality. The legitimate actors were typically hired for one-shot forays into film and, at best, appeared in films intermittently. Pilar-Morin is perhaps an exception here, but even she seems to have appeared only in special releases. In any case, these actors did not appear with anything approaching the regularity of the everyday members of the manufacturer's stock companies. Florence Lawrence, for instance, was reported to appear in three hundred roles a year.[1] This claim is exaggerated, but the fact that it could be made is significant. Because of her regular, if not constant, appearance in films, she encouraged a different type of reading than did the renowned theatrical stars.

A final difference between the theatrical stars and the picture personality has to be noted, if only in passing. The theatrical stars were, in general, much older than the picture personalities that began to become prominent in 1910. This is especially true for the female picture personalities, most of whom were in their teens. Pilar-Morin must have seemed terribly out of place as the Edison star, ostensibly competing with these teenagers. Whatever the case, it seems that the cinema, once it began to develop and promote its own stars, was much more intent on basing it on a cult of youth than the theater had been.

The picture personality's fame thus stemmed primarily from his or her appearance in films, not from previous theater work; the picture personality was a movie star, not a theatrical star appearing on film. Accepting this definition provisionally, we can begin to discuss the early promotions of picture personalities. Most writers have at this point moved directly to the Imp promotion of Florence Lawrence as the first effort in this direction. There were, however, similar promotions carried out by other companies throughout 1909 and early 1910.

At least three companies were involved in these efforts: Kalem, Edison, and Pathé. Perhaps the earliest effort to publicize film actors was made by Kalem. In January of 1909, a photograph of the Kalem Stock Company appeared in *The New York Dramatic Mirror*, and underneath was a list of all of the players' names.[2] The appearance of this photograph is extraordinary considering the amount of time it would take before other companies would make similar gestures. A year later Kalem made another innovation by offering exhibitors a poster for lobby display presenting eleven individual photographs of its stock company. This time no names were included. An article in *Moving Picture World* announcing this innovation noted the exhibitor's need for such advertising:

> Managers of picture theaters and nickelodeons all over the country are making repeated urgent requests upon the producers of moving picture subjects for photographs of the principal actresses and actors taking part in them. Heretofore requests of this character have come from love-smitten patrons of the places. The managers of the places now see a big advertising advantage in the display of such photographs in the lobbies of their theaters. The idea is an old one in the theater field and would more than make good in the picture field.[3]

The Edison Company was quite active in publicizing its actors during 1909 as well. Much of the publicity, as noted earlier, centered on the film appearances of Pilar-Morin. Yet, a substantial amount, while certainly continuing the discourse on acting, singled out actors who were not clearly known to the public as famous actors. In late 1909, for instance, two issues of *The Edison Kinetogram* published full cast lists for its current releases.[4] It also included, in three issues beginning September 15, a feature entitled "Our Stock Company," which presented a picture of an actor in the company and a brief description, such as the following one for Herbert Bostwick:

> Herbert Bostwick, the second member of our gallery of players to be introduced to the readers of the Kinetogram, is an actor of sterling worth whose twelve years of dramatic experience, eight of which have been under the critical eye of that wizard of the stage, David Belasco, has made him an actor who knows every heart throb and dramatic thrill that can be drawn out of a situation. Reserved power and clean, clear-cut artistic work place Mr. Bostwick, as a man of rare abilities, among our gallery of players, and one whom any manager would be proud to have in his cast.[5]

William Sorelle, who had been the first Edison actor featured in "Our Stock Company," appeared on the cover of *The Kinetogram* in December, along with the caption "William J. Sorelle as Mephistopheles in 'Faust.'" During this time the Edison Company became the first company to announce the cast of their pictures on the screen.[6] There is no doubt that this kind of publicity was reserved for what Edison considered its quality films. And, in this sense, all of these efforts can be seen as a simple continuation of the discourse on acting, an attempt to associate the Edison films with the aesthetic legitimacy of the theater. But many of the actors that the Edison company promoted toward the end of 1909 did not bring any theatrical fame with them to the screen; their fame would stem from their appearances in Edison films and from the Edison publicity. They were transitional figures, no doubt, but they were nevertheless promoted as picture personalities.

An interesting and, in my mind, very telling example of the shift toward the promotion of picture personalities can be seen in the efforts of the Pathé Film D'Art in the beginning of 1910. As noted in the previous chapter, Pathé had, in the previous year, been assiduously promoting well-known French actors' appearances in film. In February 1910 *Moving Picture World* published what seemed to be a continuation of this tack, a photograph of and article about Mlle. Victoria Lepanto, who was appearing in a filmed version of *Carmen*. [7] There were a number of differences between this promotion and the earlier ones of the Film D'Art, however. First, the article was actually entitled "Picture Personalities: Victoria Lepanto." Related to this, but undoubtedly more important, is the fact that nothing in the fairly lengthy article referred to Lepanto as having a theatrical background of any kind. Lepanto was, as the article claimed the accompanying photograph proved, "ordained by nature" to play the part of Carmen. There is no mention of her artistic qualifications. In fact, the only reference to her past was that she had appeared in the role of Marguerite Gautier in *The Lady with the Camelias*, another Pathé film. This is a clear departure from the promotions of Severin, LeBargy, and LeLaune. Lepanto was being promoted and received as a picture personality:

In regard to the personalities of the moving picture stage, Pathes have a great opportunity to make public the identities of the artists who work for them, because Pathes are one of the greatest moving picture houses in the world. They have gone after the talent, and the talent which works for them properly looks for the reward of publicity for its efforts. This favorably reacts on commercial exploiters of talent. It all comes to this: that just as the public has very properly interested itself in the personality of Mme. Pilar-Morin, it will also interest itself in that of Mme. Lepanto. It is interesting itself in the personalities of all of the great performers on the moving picture stage. We are glad to congratulate Pathes upon having secured the services of this charming actress. [8]

The Orpheum Theater, Oklahoma City, Oklahoma. (*Moving Picture World*, Feb. 24, 1912)

Sarah Bernhardt in *Queen Elizabeth*. (The Museum of Modern Art, Film Stills Archive)

We Nail a Lie

The blackest and at the same time the silliest lie yet circulated by enemies of the "Imp" was the story foisted on the public of St. Louis last week to the effect that Miss Lawrence (the "Imp" girl, formerly known as the "Biograph" girl) had been killed by a street car. It was a black lie because so cowardly. It was a silly lie because so easily disproved. Miss Lawrence was not even in a street-car accident, is in the best of health, will continue to appear in "Imp" films, and very shortly some of the best work in her career is to be released. We now announce our next films:

"The Broken Bath"
(Released March 14th.   Length 950 feet.)

"We Nail a Lie." (The Museum of Modern Art, Film Stills Archive)

Carlyle Blackwell. (Billy Rose
Theatre Collection, The New York
Public Library at Lincoln Center,
Astor, Lenox, and Tilden Foun-
dations)

Florence Turner. (Billy Rose
Theatre Collection, The New York
Public Library at Lincoln Center,
Astor, Lenox, and Tilden Foun-
dations)

Vitagraph Poster. (Hoblitzelle Theatre Arts Collection, University of Texas, Austin)

Florence Lawrence. (The Museum of Modern Art, Film Stills Archive)

Alice Joyce. (The Museum of Modern Art, Film Stills Archive)

Mary Fuller. (The Museum of Modern Art, Film Stills Archive)

Francis X. Bushman. (The Museum of Modern Art, Film Stills Archive)

The problem with most of the previous writing on the early star system is that in stressing the singular and supposedly initiatory appeal of Florence Lawrence it has ignored the broader context within which actors became well known. To note this fault is not to consign the Lawrence promotion to the margins of film history, however. It was certainly the most masterful, and probably the most significant, early promotion. An account of Lawrence's rise to fame and her subsequent fortunes as an actor in many ways exemplifies the work of the burgeoning publicity apparatus. At least two points must be kept in mind when approaching this account, though: first, the Lawrence promotion cannot be seen in isolation from the other promotions of the day; and second, Lawrence cannot be seen, for whatever reason, as the origin of the star system.

Florence Lawrence began film acting at the end of 1906 during the period when the major film companies were first starting to build stock companies and initiate the shift toward a more rationalized production system. She contracted with the Biograph company and began to appear regularly in films. During this time Lawrence began to be recognized from film to film by avid moviegoers; she received at least one fan letter, dated December 17, 1908:

Dear Sir:
As I am a regular patron of your moving pictures in my city I would deem it a kind favor if you will tell me the name and address of the young lady in the following pictures: "The Reckoning," "The Ingrate," "After Many Years." My reason for asking the above information was the outcome of a wager that I did not have the courage to form an acquaintance with this young lady.[9]

Lawrence apparently remained with Biograph until sometime in 1909. Alexander Walker has argued that Lawrence was fired from Biograph for trying to negotiate a better contract with another company; she was then, he argues, banned from working for any of the other trust companies, and at that time that meant being out of work. Walker does not cite his sources, and I have not found anything to directly substantiate this claim. However, a letter to Lawrence from her mother in August 1910 indicates that Lawrence did consider other offers while at the Biograph and that Biograph "felt sore" about it.[10]

In any case, in the last half of 1909 Lawrence signed on with the Imp company. Imp was the creation of Carl Laemmle, a Chicago distributor who rejected his affiliation with the Motion Picture Patents Company and in 1909 became the leading figure in the independent film movement. His Laemmle Film Service depended almost wholly on renting films produced by other independents (consolidated under the banner of the International Projecting and Producing Company) until March 1909 when Laemmle announced that he was creating his own production company. An announcement in *Moving Picture World* stated that the company would "make a tremendous specialty of American subjects" and would pay the highest salaries to secure the best scripts and technicians. Although actors were not mentioned, it seems that Imp was extremely generous with Lawrence's salary; her contract reportedly guaranteed her a salary of $15,000 a year for life.[11]

The first evidence of publicity efforts centered on Lawrence appeared in *Moving Picture World* in December 1909.[12] Lawrence's picture appeared in the top corner of an ad for the film *Lest We Forget*; written across the top of the ad in boldface was "She's an Imp!" Although Lawrence's name was not mentioned, the ad clearly traded on an identity that had already been constructed through the dozens of films Lawrence had appeared in over the years. It is this identity that the early fan letters to Lawrence refer to. Two of these letters must be typical. The first was handed to the manager of a St. Louis theater with the following note attached: "To the manager: Kindly hand this to the lady who is known as "Flo" in "Love's Strategem."

Dear Miss Flo,
I am a young Miss 13 years old. I am very fond of the Moving Picture shows, especially fond of the Biographs, but I see you have left that company and gone with the IMP Moving Picture Company. I wish you much success and know you

will please everybody because you always have. The applause was great the other night when you appeared in "Love's Strategem." I only know you by your stage name but hope you will get this letter alright.[13]

The second was from a boy in San Francisco:

Dear Stranger,
I missed you in the AB Company and I wondered what became of you until to night for the first time I saw you in "Love's Strategem" in the Imp Company. I fully enjoy seeing you act in your cute way more so than I did any others of the AB's and I felt partly sorry when you ceased to appear in any of them. Your acting is very realistic in many ways mostly the way you make love. The first picture I ever saw you in was "His First Biscuits" do you remember the day you posed for it, gee I would like to know. I am jest 16 so there is no danger of flirtation. I jest like you and would feel highly honored if you would answer this crazy letter.

. . .

Will you please answer this letter, a postal will do, just telling me your name, your name not a stage one. You look like my sister but she is not so pretty. If you send me your name and address I will send you my picture. Write me if you see fit to.

Mister Leland Ayers
Yours truly,
Lovy Ayers

P.S. Please write and tell me you received this if you won't give me your name and address.
"Do onto others as you would wish them to do unto you."
Proverb[14]

A fan letter from Baltimore in February of the next year addressed Lawrence by name.[15] This suggests that by then there had been more specific publicity disseminated about Lawrence, probably through local papers or local exhibitors. The famous publicity stunt of the next month must thus be seen in relation to earlier, more modest, but perhaps equally calculated, moves on Imp's part. The December ad in particular demonstrates that Imp recognized Lawrence's marketability early and was intent on capitalizing on it.

The promotion of March 1910 represented a marked escalation of publicity about Lawrence. It consisted of four or perhaps five "events." First, there was ostensibly a report published in the *St. Louis Post-Dispatch* that Florence Lawrence had been killed in a streetcar accident in New York. A picture supposedly accompanied the article so that the public, who did not generally know Lawrence's name, would recognize her as one of their favorites and feel the loss. No evidence of the existence of this article has ever been produced. It is not in the *Post-Dispatch,* nor was the death mentioned in the trade press when it "happened." It seems likely that the report was trumped up as well as the accident.

The second aspect of the promotion referred back to this report and denied it. The most spectacular denial appeared in an ad in *Moving Picture World* on March 5, 1910. Lawrence's picture was prominently displayed and above it, in boldface, was "WE NAIL A LIE." Below the picture and the Imp logo was the following statement:

> The blackest and at the same time the silliest lie yet circulated by enemies of the "Imp" was the story foisted on the public of St. Louis last week to the effect that Miss Lawrence (the "Imp" girl, formerly known as the "Biograph" girl) had been killed by a street car. It was a black lie because so cowardly. It was a silly lie because so easily disproved. Miss Lawrence was not even in a street-car accident, is in the best of health, will continue to appear in "Imp" films, and very shortly some of the best work of her career is to be released. [16]

The next day in the *Sunday Magazine* of the *St. Louis Post-Dispatch* there was an article entitled "Heroes and Heroines of Moving Picture Shows," which asked who the most famous American actress was.

After dismissing Adams, Marlowe, and Barrymore, the article provided the answer:

> There is one actress playing in the silent drama, who is seen acting every night in every week simultaneously in the theaters in nearly every town in every state in the Union whose face is known to 10,000 people to the one who knows Maude Adams. Her name is Florence Lawrence, and she is a member of the stock company of a New York firm of moving picture film manufacturers. A few days ago the newspapers printed a report that she had been killed by a car in New York, and for the first time her picture was shown in the public prints. She was at once recognized as a favorite of the "canned drama" and deep regret was expressed everywhere that she would be seen no more on the screen of the picture show. But the report turned out to be a canard, the third that had been sent out by a rival of the filmmaker who is so fortunate as to control her services as an actress.[17]

If the initial report (or reports) of Lawrence's death did exist, it is ludicrous to believe that it was the fabrication of a rival film company (and that that film company provided the newspapers with a photograph of Lawrence). The whole episode clearly bears the mark of the Imp publicists. In fact, the claim that rival (read MPPC) film companies were behind this "lie" fits in very neatly with the tack of most of the other Imp and Laemmle Film Service advertising of the day—it characterized Laemmle as a benevolent and spirited Independent whose every move was opposed by the corrupt, greedy forces of the Motion Picture Patents Company.

The oddest thing about the *Post-Dispatch* article is that while it seems to single out Lawrence as the most famous actress in the world, it only spends three paragraphs of a very long article discussing her work. And it does not include a picture of this most recognizable of faces, even though it includes eleven pictures of other actors. Was a photograph of her not available? (This of course would cast doubt on the claim made in the same article that the papers had published a photograph of her earlier with her death notice). Or was this a clever way of building up the mystique surrounding her name?

The article goes on to discuss the work of Pilar-Morin, Rolinda Bainbridge, Bernadine Reisse, and Ethel Jewett, all of the Edison Stock Company, and it also lists and provides pictures of members of the Selig and Lubin stock companies. The MPPC companies were certainly as active as Imp in providing information for the article. The Lawrence promotion was obviously not, in substance, as innovative as film history has led us to believe.

On March 19 of the same year another ad appeared in *Moving Picture World* that referred to Lawrence, this time through the reproduction of a letter supposedly written by an appreciative exhibitor in San Diego:

> Dear Imp—As manager of dramatic companies for over 26 years, I wish to express my appreciation of the splendid stagecraft in evidence in all IMP productions. You not only have a superb acting company, but at long distance I take my hat off to your stage director. My audience cry for IMPS and go into ecstasies over the artistic work of Miss Lawrence and your handsome and talented leading man. I can assure you your enterprise and liberality are appreciated all over the Pacific Coast, for you do things well.[18]

The next element of the promotion appeared the next day in the *St. Louis Post-Dispatch,* in an article entitled "The Girl of a Thousand Faces."[19] It focused entirely on Lawrence and included pictures of her in many different dramatic poses, each of which represented a particular emotion: sadness, determination, piety, horror, hilarity, etc. The title referred both to her acting ability (her ability to strike all of these poses) and to the fact that because of the reproducibility of her image, she could appear at a thousand theaters at once. The article included comments by Lawrence on the art of film acting, on the fan letters she had received, and on the crowds that gathered to watch the filmmaking process. The article contradicts the March 6 report that a picture was published with Lawrence's death notice by stating that it was publishing the first photographs in a newspaper of Lawrence. In fact it says that people did not really pay much attention to the article about the actress's death, because they could not recognize her by her name alone. There is not much respect for consistency in these articles, much less truth.

The final event in this promotion was a visit to St. Louis in April by Lawrence, her co-star King Baggot (who had conveniently gained recognition in St. Louis the previous summer in a play), H. L. Salter, her director and husband, and Thomas Cochrane, the manager of the company and the person responsible for most of the Imp publicity. A *Moving Picture World* article stated that the report of the death of Lawrence had so upset her admirers in St. Louis that "nothing short of seeing her in the flesh would satisfy them":

> The Imp actors will give a stage demonstration of moving pictures in the making and their St. Louis friends have arranged for a grand reception. Mr. Cochrane takes with him a film showing how the reading of Miss Lawrence's obituary notice affected the other members of the Imp Company. If anyone can see the hand of the press agent in this, that person must at least be credited with a clever and original idea. And Miss Lawrence is a clever girl and is worthy of the attention she has attracted.[20]

The actor's visit to the moving picture theater would be a popular gimmick in the years to come.

Lawrence probably did emerge as the most popular film actor during these early years, though like most of the early "stars" her popularity was not long lived. This can be explained in part by the various career twists and interruptions that followed her initial success. By the summer of 1910 both Lawrence and her husband, Harry Salter, were fighting with Cochrane. In August, Salter wrote Lawrence the following letter:

> Cochrane has got on my nerves and I am going to have it out with him today. I am going to tell him we will quit the 1st of September. We will take the chance and go somewhere else. We can go to England and get a job as they want us there. We

can try Lubin first and if there is any trouble we can do the other. What do you say to a trip to Europe? This pain is too much with the IMP. If I had some assistance it wouldn't be so bad. But this continually bucking Cochrane is too much. He told Giles not to take any orders from me, only he and Miss O'Kief.[21]

The Lubin offer was for $300 a week, substantially the same salary Lawrence had supposedly received at Imp. On August 9, her mother wrote, "Cochrane feels sore at your considering any other propositions. Just like the Biograph. He thinks he has done wonders for you and doubtless feels injured." Lawrence and Salter sailed for Europe aboard the steamship *Merion* on September 10, 1910.[22] The next month Imp published Lawrence's photograph, and the following announcement in *Moving Picture World:*

> To stop, once for all time, the silly rumors to effect that Miss Florence Lawrence is working for some other film manufacturer, the "Imp" company publishes the fact that its contract with Miss Lawrence does not expire until a year from next March. Even if we wished to let her go, or if she wished to leave the "Imp" Company, it could not be done, as the contract provides that neither party can break it or violate any of its conditions. This ought to settle the doubts of all who may have become confused by the rumors they have heard.[23]

The doubts of course had been well founded. The next month Lawrence was listed as a member of the Lubin stock company. Imp brought a lawsuit up against Lawrence for breach of contract and mounted a counteroffensive by focusing its publicity efforts on another actor, Mary Pickford. In December a very large picture of Pickford and an accompanying article appeared in *Moving Picture World.*[24] Like Lawrence, Pickford had become a recognizable figure in Biograph films before being hired by Imp.

Lawrence was apparently not happy at Lubin. Her brother Norman wrote her in January, 1911, asking her, "Don't the Lubin people treat you as agreed or is it just the law suit the Imp is having with you that worries you so much? I should think the Lubin would fight your law suit, and pay you as they were the first ones to tempt you to leave." In February, after less than five months at Lubin, she quit the company and "sailed away for a long rest." A letter from her mother indicates that she had fallen into ill health; it is possible that her "worries" led to a nervous breakdown.[25]

When she returned from her trip in May, Lawrence signed a contract with P. A. Powers that, in effect, formed a new, independent film company for her to act in—Victor Films.[26] Her husband Harry would be the director, and the films would be distributed as part of the Universal program (ironically, the president of Universal was Carl Laemmle). Although Owen Moore co-starred in the Victor films, the company was clearly designed to capitalize on Lawrence's fame. In fact, a cameo bearing a representation of Lawrence's face served as the company's trademark. Lawrence had the option of returning to Lubin if the Victor venture did not work out; however, there are indications that both Victor and Lubin offered her a salary below that she had received prior to her self-imposed rest.[27]

As the following letter from her mother indicates, Lawrence was almost immediately unhappy:

> Well dear, I am sorry that you are so unhappy. As you say truly that it will not do for you to jump this job as it will look as tho you are not trustworthy. Still, the firm is looking for your name to pull them through and you are taking less money than you can get elsewhere. . . . I hope that Harry will be able to furnish up-to-date good picture material for your work so that you can still show your countless supporters that you are it and in the fact at the head. You mean so much to him in a financial way. No matter what he says about it you were it before he was director and still are, so make the most of your present position in a financial way.[28]

She quit Victor in the spring of 1913, supposedly to devote herself to "rose culture."[29] But in August she was lured back to make a series of two- and three-reel films with her husband. The first one premiered on October 3. Advertisements touted Lawrence as "the highest salaried actress in the moving picture field" and announced that because of the incredible expense of the films she was appearing in, exchanges would have to charge higher prices:

> Regardless of the cost, get every Florence Lawrence feature released! Not only are they perfect gems, but Miss Lawrence's photograph shown in your lobby with the announcement, "Florence Lawrence Here Today," will cause you to do a capacity business. It is up to you to grasp every golden opportunity like this the instant it comes your way. It means something to you to be able to advertise the most popular picture actress in the world![30]

Whether she was still the most popular actress in the world is open to question. She had finished fifth in a *Photoplay* reader's popularity poll in July 1913, but only thirtieth in a *Motion Picture Story Magazine* poll conducted in October.[31] Whatever the case, it is clear that the manufacturers were banking on her past popularity. Lawrence was never to regain that popularity, however. In 1916 her face was disfigured in a film accident with Arthur Johnson. But even without the accident it seems that Lawrence was destined, by the middle teens, to fade into relative obscurity like other early stars, such as Florence Turner and Mary Fuller. After only a few years these stars already seemed like part of a bygone era.

Every major film company, with the exception of Biograph, made efforts to publicize its leading actors during 1910. Three of these promotions are probably the most important. The first, which focused on Vitagraph actress Florence Turner, most closely paralleled the Lawrence promotion, though it began shortly after it. Turner, like Lawrence, had certainly become a recognizable figure by early 1910 because of her many appearances in a single company's films. Lawrence had been known as "The Biograph Girl"; Turner was known as "The Vitagraph Girl." In April 1910 Vitagraph began promoting its regular stock company in earnest when it offered exhibitors a poster for lobby display similar to the one Kalem had produced three months earlier. In July, a long article on Turner appeared in *Moving Picture World* in the section "Picture Person-alities" (the second installment of the section that had begun with the piece on Victoria Lepanto).[32] A large photograph of Turner, in the role of Edna in *St. Elmo,* accompanied the article, which was presented as the story of the author's visit to the Vitagraph Studios to track down "the famous Vitagraph girl":

> For we had read, we had heard of her, we had seen her picture, and the mental conception that we had formed of her was of Juno-like dignity and other charming feminine attributes one likes to associate with the personality of a graceful player of that sex to which it is our misfortune not to belong. But, bless you, Miss Turner is no Juno, no Amazon, she is petite, dark, slender, vivacious, full of life and go, just as we see her on the stage, a right lively, good-natured and popular little woman, beloved by all the members of that very happy family which works at the Vitagraph studio, just as she is admired and adored by the millions of people who look upon her counterfeit presentment on the moving picture screen.[33]

There were, as the above quotation indicates, certainly publicity efforts that focused specifically on Turner prior to this article. Turner had at least been making personal appearances at theaters in the Brooklyn area. The first of these appearances noted in *Moving Picture World* was in April:

> A very novel treat was afforded the attendances at Saratoga Park, Brooklyn, moving picture parlor last Saturday eve-ning. A reception was tendered Miss Florence Turner, known as "The Vitagraph Girl," by Manager Robertson and a special exhibition of Vitagraph pictures was given. The thea-ter was crowded to the fullest capacity. When the title page of "The Vitagraph Girl" song was thrown on the screen, the applause was deafening, but just as soon as Eddy Warden began to sing her charms as the song slides displayed them, the audience was admiring and patiently waiting for the

chorus in which they all joined with a right good will and they demanded an encore so they could sing it again. Miss Turner was introduced by a Vitagraph representative. After the applause subsided, she responded in a very naive and fetching little speech. The approval was instantaneous. Her admirers were not satisfied until she acknowledged their appreciation by accepting a magnificent bouquet of flowers.[34]

In July, another Turner appearance was noted:

On Tuesday and Wednesday evenings, June 28 and 29, Miss Florence E. Turner, "The Vitagraph Girl," was given a Vitagraph reception at the "Fulton Auditorium," Fulton street and Nostrand Avenue, Brooklyn N.Y. It is generally the case when a "Vitagraph Night" is given the place where it is given is packed to the street, and these two were no exception, and the enthusiasm was a gratification to the managers and exceedingly complimentary to "The Vitagraph Girl," who in addition to the hearty applause which sounded her welcome was the recipient of a number of beautiful floral pieces.[35]

It seems that such personal appearances were a regular feature of "Vitagraph Night." In any case, such appearances were not uncommon. At the end of 1910 another Turner appearance was noted in *Moving Picture World*—"Vitagraph Girl Night at the Academy":

Truly it was a revelation. That those who pose for the Silent Drama gain a tangible hold on their audiences we were aware. That the popularity of the Shadow Girl would cause a small riot by reason of the eagerness of those who knew only the "shadow" to greet the reality was, to say the least, a surprise. In a way, too, it was an enlightening illustration, or demonstration, of the hold the moving picture itself has upon the public.[36]

On January 6, 1911, The Newspaper Enterprise Association, a feature syndicate, included a photograph of Turner in its daily birthday feature, which had previously included "only national figures, jurists, educators and divines."[37] Turner was definitely one of the most publicized and one of the most popular film actors of these early years. Her marketability is highlighted in the following advice about how to use photoplayers in film advertising: "Play up the personality of the players. It is possible to get slides of many if not all of the favorites. Use these to build up business. If you had Sarah Bernhardt booked for next week you would tell them she was coming. Run a slide that you've a Vitagraph coming with Miss Turner, and then flash Miss Turner's slide. It is more than doubly effective. You can find from the Vitagraph bulletin when Miss Turner appears."[38]

Toward the end of 1911, Turner became ill from overexhaustion and had to stop making films to take a rest; in May 1912 she returned to Vitagraph. However, early in 1913 she quit Vitagraph and appeared briefly in vaudeville. In March there was an announcement that Turner, "the first real photoplay star," was going to England to produce her own films. The company she formed was called Turner Films. According to Anthony Slide, Turner appeared in around thirty productions there. A few of them, such as *My Old Dutch*, were international successes, but when World War I severely crippled the British film industry Turner was forced to return to the United States. At first she got occasional starring roles in minor pictures, but her career soon began to fall apart, and for the next twenty years she had to struggle to continue acting in bit parts.[39]

Although Marion Leonard had appeared in films previously at Biograph, and was perhaps already a recognized figure, the first publicity in the trades that concerned her appeared in an announcement of the founding of Reliance films, produced by the Carlton Motion Picture Laboratories.[40] A large picture of Leonard was set in the bottom left-hand corner of the ad with the caption "Marion Leonard, Leading Woman." The ad is even more hyperbolic than most, but the stock company led by Leonard did include the names of four other actors who would become extremely popular early stars: James Kirkwood, Arthur Johnson, Henry Walthall, and Phillips Smalley. I have not determined how long Leonard remained with Reliance, only that she disappeared from filmmaking prior to an extensive promotional campaign signaling her association with another new company, Gem, which intended to base its success on Leonard's popularity. The Leonard/Gem promotions are, in retrospect, the most clever of the period. The promotion began with a picture published in both *Moving Picture News* and *Moving Picture World* (occupying a full-page spread in the latter) of Leonard's face framed by a diamond ring. Underneath the picture was the intriguing caption "Marion Leonard Engaged."[41]

The week after this ad appeared in *The Moving Picture News*, another ad was published, "A Message from the Stars to the Brightest One of Them." The message appeared under a picture of Leonard, suspended in the heavens, with her head bursting through a star:

> Twinkle, Twinkle, Little Star
> How we wonder where you are!
> Up above our salaries so high—
> Will you tell us by and by?
>   *   *   *
> And Echo answers, "Where?"[42]

This question was answered in both *Moving Picture World* and *Moving Picture News* in the next two weeks when the nature of Leonard's "engagement" was explained in a full-page ad consisting of a letter from the actor:

> People—I am engaged! Cupid's (not Cupidity's) arrow finally hit the target! Many suitors and wooers I've had—modesty forbids me to specify the number. There's one born every minute, but one particular minute about sixteen years ago (now, stop laughing!) it so happened that one was not born. "Mari" was "on" and didn't want to weight herself with a burden whose greatest asset was its own load. So—I just weighted! Until—a Gem came along! Yes, everybody, the Gem Motion Picture Co. captured my heart, as it will yours. Its aim was true—and its aim by the way, is to give the bestest

and brightest in pictorial art. I hope—and predict—you're going to like us.

    I'm theirs—and yours
      Truly,
      Marion Leonard[43]

There was an extraordinary amount of publicity about the upcoming Gem films—an interview with Leonard in *Moving Picture News,* and, later, a three-page article on the first Gem releases. The latter called the films soon to be released "nothing less than wonderful," and one of the films in particular was pronounced "the best film . . . we have seen in our entire extensive and varied acquaintance with moving pictures." Something happened to the Gem Company before they could release these films, however. The day before Gem was to release their first picture another company, Rex, announced that it had bought all twenty-six of the negatives to the "famous Marion Leonard 'Gems,'" and that it would release them as a second weekly release.[44] The next month Leonard was being touted in ads as the foremost actor in moving pictures:

> SARAH BERNHARDT is the foremost living female interpreter of human emotions on the stage today. The general consensus of opinion signifies that Charlotte Walker, Grace George, Julia Marlowe, Ethel Barrymore, Margaret Illington, and a host of other favorites only approach SARAH! Without any doubt, without any question, without any reasonable refutation, the greatest interpreter of human emotions in the moving picture field is MARION LEONARD! That's the conclusion at which the exhibitors of the country are arriving via the REX MARION LEONARD SUNDAY RELEASES. They route all others.[45]

That same month there was an article in *Moving Picture World* detailing Rex's plans for its second year and featuring photographs of Marion Leonard and, on a second page, the other players who "had made Rex famous." That year Rex joined Universal; thus Leonard began to appear on the same program as Florence Lawrence, King Baggot, and Owen Moore.[46]

Mary Pickford, like Lawrence, Turner, and Leonard, had appeared in dozens of films before her name began to be explicitly publicized. Her association with Biograph had, to some degree, assured her anonymity though she had become known to most of the patrons of Biograph films as "Little Mary." She became the subject of a publicity campaign only after she left Biograph and was hired to work for Imp. As noted earlier, in December 1910 a full-page spread appeared on Pickford in *Moving Picture World,* complete with an extremely large photograph:

> Miss Pickford is an artiste of the highest rank in a field where there are few of her kind. She is one of three brilliant stars in the motion picture firmament, rising to the top of her profession while yet too young to sign a contract. Preceding her photoplay experience she so pleased Mr. Belasco in "The Warrens of Virginia" that she received high approval and encouragement from that discoverer of native talent. Her success with another picture company was so pronounced that she became known to millions as "Little Mary."[47]

Her first appearance with Imp was in *Their First Misunderstanding,* released January 9, 1911. It was the first of a long series of films publicized as the "Little Mary Imps." Pickford's name typically did not accompany ads for these films; she was simply referred to as "Little Mary," as was the character she played. A picture of her co-star and husband Owen Moore appeared in at least one of these ads with her along with the captions "He's an Imp!" and "She's an Imp!"[48]

In 1911 Thomas Cochrane, the manager of Imp and the person ostensibly responsible for its publicity, left that company and became general manager of a new company, Majestic. In October he announced that he had secured the services of Mary Pickford and Owen Moore. Imp took legal action but the court dismissed the case, ruling that Pickford's contract with Imp was not binding because she was a minor. The ads for the company's first release, *The Courting of*

Mary, prominently displayed the names and photographs of Pickford and Moore. [49]

There was no similar publicity build-up when Pickford joined Biograph again in 1912 and began making films with D. W. Griffith. The next promotion of Pickford was associated with her appearance, in early 1913, in a play at the Republic Theater in New York:

> Little Mary Holds Daily Reception
> Mary Pickford plays the blind girl Juliet in "A Good Little Devil," David Belasco's production of the beautiful fairy play by Mme. Rostand and her son. The sweet personality and beautiful face of this clever little actress are familiar all over the world to patrons of the film shows, by whom she is intimately known as "Little Mary" and "The Maude Adams of the Movies." Wherever she has appeared in the new Belasco success she has been besieged on the streets, in department stores, in fact everywhere by thousands of admirers, especially women and young girls. After every matinee performance crowds gather at the stage door of the Republic theater waiting for her to come out. [50]

Pickford's success in this production demonstrates how much the status of the film actor had changed in five years. Moving pictures had depended very heavily on the fame actors had achieved in the theater. Pickford's engagement in the Belasco play represents a significant reversal: the fame of a film star was being used to insure the success of a legitimate play. The play ran for 152 performances in New York. The usual practice would have then been to take the play on the road, but another tack was announced. Noting the impossibility of satisfying the demand from all parts of the country through a conventional theatrical tour, it was announced that "Little Mary" would again be in pictures: "Through an arrangement between Mr. Belasco and Daniel Frohman, managing director, and Adolph Zukor, president of the Famous Players, all of the wonderful scenes and effects of 'A Good Little Devil' will be shown in motion pictures." [51]

Pickford's association with Famous Players went well beyond this single project. She became, in effect, the company's leading star and went on to make such films as *Caprice* and *In the Bishop's Carriage*. Reviews focused on her work in the films and praised her lavishly. There were also long interviews with her published in both *Photoplay* and *Motography* in August. Pickford was called in one article "the most popular motion picture star in the world," and she certainly had some claim to this title though it would be hers uncontestedly in a few years. In November 1913 she moved to the new Famous Players studios in Los Angeles, under the direction of Edwin S. Porter.[52]

Although the earliest publicity for picture personalities focused on female actors, by late 1910 male actors began to receive an equal amount of attention. In December Maurice Costello, the Vitagraph "leading man" who had appeared opposite Florence Turner in such films as *St. Elmo*, was featured in the "Picture Personality" section of *Moving Picture World*. The article addressed the question of the male personalities directly:

> As our pages have evidenced for many months past, the leading ladies of the various moving picture plants, alike in respect of their personal charm and their acting abilities, have created great interest amongst the general public. Of course, the actor, as we admitted a few weeks ago, was bound to come into his own. He is sharing popularity with the actress. Just as much interest attaches to the leading man of a moving picture company amongst the fair sex, as attaches to the personality of an actress amongst men.[53]

In February 1911, Costello was given a page-and-a-half layout in the first issue of *The Motion Picture Story Magazine*, the earliest fan magazine. Costello achieved enormous popularity, as did King Baggot, the "leading man" for the Imp company, who first received publicity in connection with the Florence Lawrence visit to St. Louis. By October 1911 enormous photographs of Baggot's head dominated advertisements for the films he was in.[54] Owen Moore, as noted previously, got a great deal of publicity as Pickford's co-star at both Imp and Majestic. Francis X. Bushman began to be featured prominently in Essanay publicity in August 1911. In November 1912 Bushman quit Essanay and made a successful tour of moving picture theaters, lecturing on the art of moving pictures. Then in 1913 Essanay lured him back, supposedly with a very lucrative contract. Romaine Fielding of Solax was another actor who became well known and popular during this time, as was Warren Kerrigan of American.[55] Essanay's western star G. M. Anderson ("Bronco Billy") and Vitagraph's comedian John Bunny should be included here as well, since both were, from a very early date, extremely popular. Their generic affiliations (as well as physical attributes) denied them the status of "heartthrobs," but they were nevertheless established and marketable personalities.

One could go on almost indefinitely listing the players, both male and female, that became famous during these years and discussing the details of their promotion. This would give some indication of the size of the explosion of publicity about film actors after 1909, but it might tell us little else since the publicity from actor to actor is fairly redundant. What could be said, and thus known, about Florence Lawrence was not markedly different from what could be said about Mary Fuller or Florence LaBadie. There was undeniably something unique and specific about Florence Lawrence, something that in certain contexts would deserve a full explanation. But such an explanation would need to be based on an understanding of the regularities of discourse that produced all picture personalities. Although there was an incredible proliferation of discourse about picture personalities during this time, all of this discourse fell within a fairly narrow range, repeating certain patterns, exhibiting certain obsessions, and excluding a number of concerns that would later define the "star." Thus, at this point, it is important to turn to a more general definition of the mode of existence of the picture personality. One can delineate three aspects of the picture personality's existence in discourse: the circulation of the name; the "image," taken in the broad sense to denote both the actor's physical image and the personality that is represented as existing within or behind it; and a discourse on the actor's professional experience.

Through a dual movement of concealment and revelation, the player's name was constituted and valorized as a site of knowledge. Anthony Slide has argued that the public knew the names of the photoplayers by 1912, and this may be a conservative estimate depending on how one defines the public.[56] In any case, what this reveals is the extent and intensity of the will to knowledge that had been elicited concerning the name, since before 1909 virtually none of the players' names had been known. There is a kind of overdetermination of the hermeneutic code in the reception of films during this period, yet, this code does not stretch so much across the text as a series of questions to be answered at the text's end.[57] It was instead comprised of questions about the identity of the people appearing in films, questions that led to discourses produced outside of the fiction. At its most basic level, these questions led to and were answered by a name, an identification in a quite literal sense. That name, in turn, became the necessary support for any further elaboration of the actor's identity.

The early fan magazines depended to a large extent on the pleasure the public took in knowing the players' names. Such features as *Moving Picture Story Magazine*'s "Prize Puzzle Contest" offered prizes to those who could fill in the blanks of a story with the names of photoplayers. One of the stories, for instance, included the line "Once he had been a ——— in deepest Africa." The answer was "Bushman," as in Francis X. Bushman. The next year, the same magazine's "Popular Player Puzzle" included puzzles such as "A favorite pet of the children." The answer—John Bunny.[58]

It is appropriate that the actors' names were included in puzzles, because that is how they were received more generally, as something to be figured out, pieced together from film to film. Once one knew the names of players one could exercise that knowledge by writing what were called "appreciations":

> King Baggott of them all is "King"
> And he rules on the silver screen.
> Every time I know he's to be on the show
> I put on my bonnett and off I go.
>
> For Kenneth Casey—
> There's a lad with the Vitagraph that we all adore
> When we see him once we want to see him more.[59]

These appreciations involved naming a player's name and stating how much he or she was admired. They were counted as votes in *The Motion Picture Story Magazine's* "Popular Player Contest."[60] *Photoplay* and *The Ladies World* had similar contests, each based on identifying a favorite actor by name.[61] The fan magazines also had question-and-answer sections that were geared largely toward providing curious readers with the names of the actors in their favorite films. Here are two typical answers:

> Emery C., Chicago—Yes, the "Little Red Riding Hood" of the Majestic company was enacted by Mary Pickford, who formerly appeared in the Imp films. She is now in the employ of the Biograph company. (2) Florence LaBadie was the "Juliet" of Thanhouser's "Romeo and Juliet."
>
> SOME CHANGES—To avoid a flood of inquiries, we announce these changes before they become apparent in the pictures. John R. Compson, from Edison to Imp, Herbert Prior and Mabel Trunelle, from Edison to Majestic. Grace Lewis, Vitagraph to Imp. Make a note, please, and do not repeat these inquiries.[62]

The fan magazines show the most striking evidence of this emphasis on the actors' names, but it is probably in film exhibition that the names were circulated to the greatest effect. Posters, as we shall see later, advertised the names of actors appearing in films "inside" theaters; reproductions of articles from the trades about specific actors could be made and posted outside; slides could be obtained depicting and naming actors and projected in the theater before the film; and, finally, cast lists could be provided, either in paper form or within the films themselves.

As noted earlier, Edison was credited in 1909 with being the first company to present the casts of its best pictures on the screen.[63] In 1910 *Moving Picture World* responded to a letter requesting more information about actors in the magazine by stating that it would like to provide more information but that the major manufacturers withheld the necessary information for them to do so. It then offered the following suggestion:

We suggest the step, however, which, if taken, will, we think, meet our correspondent's desire and be for the good of the business in that it will emphasize public interest in these moving picture actors and actresses, whose personalities are certainly as interesting as those of the people on the ordinary stage. Let each picture or reel be preceded by the full cast of the characters in the play, with the names of the actors and actresses playing the parts. This being done, the people in a theater will soon get to know these actors' and actresses' names, and so will we. We shall be able to follow their doings on the screen, just as if we were criticizing plays in an ordinary theater where programs are provided. Then would be our opportunity to analyze and criticize the acting in these picture plays by singling out various actors and actresses for mention. [64]

The next year a letter to *Moving Picture World* from an exhibitor signaled the need for producers to name the cast. The editor replied that "Edison, Pathe, Gaumont, Eclair, Great Northern, Vitagraph and others" were already introducing the leading characters at the beginning of "important reels." [65] This is not a large percentage of the manufacturers that were active in 1911, but it does seem that screen credits began to become common practice around this time. An article from September entitled "The Artists of the Screen" claimed that the actor was finally "coming into his own, and getting his name under the film-titles and his photograph into reputable magazines and into the gilt frames that decorate the lobby of every up-to-date photoplay house." The credit was "the best evidence of the increasing sanity of the filmmakers." *Photoplay* could claim in late 1912 that the idea of credits for actors on the screen was "fiercely attacked by several." There was certainly some debate about whether the cast lists should be presented on the screen or printed in programs, after a theatrical model. [66] And there were supposedly those who did not believe that the casts should be presented at all.

The argument that the manufacturers were reluctant to reveal the names of their actors is at the base of most histories of the early star system. According to most, there was a strong clash between the studios' efforts to suppress the emergence of picture personalities and the public's desire to know about them, one that was finally resolved in favor of the public. It is difficult to imagine that the manufacturers lost this clash; what they in fact won was a massive audience eager to "consume" the latest star. In fact, from the evidence presented to this point, one would have to doubt that such a clash even existed; the manufacturers were promoting their players from a very early date. However, this argument cannot merely be dismissed as a wrong-headed historical explanation, because it appeared concurrently with the picture personalities themselves; it was thus a part of the events I am attempting to explain and must itself be explained.

Three major reasons have been given to explain the studios' reluctance to supply the public with their players' names. The first is the rationale that was offered most frequently by the manufacturers. It contended that the players were, in reality, serious actors from the legitimate stage and that they did not want their names revealed because they feared their involvement in moving pictures would ruin their professional reputation. As Anthony Slide has pointed out, this rationale can hardly account for the widespread concealment of the players' names. Almost all of the early actors came from provincial stock companies, not Broadway. Few had much of a reputation to lose.[67] But statements such as the following appeared frequently: "I can't tell you about the wonderful people that posed for Mr. Selig in picture dramas. That is a secret—now. If I could only give you the names! Nine great names have played at the plant!"[68] The work of legitimization effected through this rationale is perhaps obvious, yet one must admire its thoroughgoingness. The public did not know the name of a given picture personality, but this ignorance could be explained; it was ostensibly because she or he was a great actor, or at least one with a reputation. The irony of this, of course, is that the names of the well-known actors who entered film acting were clearly not concealed—they were heralded. No evidence has ever been un-covered to suggest that any legitimate actor of note ever appeared in a film during this period without publicity. By implying that the actors they did not publicize were famous and by publicizing their famous actors, the manufacturers could have it both ways. These two tacks fit in very well with the larger strategy of legitimization effected through the discourse on acting.

A second explanation for the studios' efforts to conceal the players' names is largely economic, or, to be more accurate, it centered on the interface between film as a commodity and film as a form of enunciation. How would film as a product be differentiated? And how would the subject of enunciation be figured? These questions were answered only through a struggle over which aspect of film production would emerge for the consumer as the principal site of textual productivity. Frank Woods's short history of the star system specifies the terms of this struggle. "It was one of the beliefs of the combination [the Patents Company] that they would avoid the troubles of the theatrical managers—big salaries to the stars and players—by rigidly concealing the names of the actors and actresses. They would play up only the names of the manufacturing companies and the public would never—no never—be the wiser."[69] This desire to have the audience associate a film with a company rather than an individual was behind Biograph's policy to keep its actors anonymous—or so *Moving Picture World* claimed when it announced that Biograph was dropping this policy:

> Officials of the Biograph Company have never deigned to give an explanation of their rule which forbade announcements concerning the identity of members of their several companies. Report has it that the reason is explained by a theory that the Biograph company is an institution and an entity; that the Biograph quality depends upon no individual, but is unchanging from year to year no matter who may come and go; and that to feature any individual in connection with the pictures would detract something from the name of Biograph as an idea.[70]

In the last chapter I noted that articles such as "The Cinematographer and Some of His Difficulties" and some of the early discussions of film acting marked a certain shift in discourse toward an emphasis on the human labor involved in film production. This shift was not immediate nor uncontested, however. It undoubtedly seemed like there were financial benefits to be gained from the anonymity of directors, photoplaywrights, and actors. As late as 1909 there was a claim that all regular members of a stock company got the same pay—five dollars a day. The manufacturers could, by focusing all of their efforts on gaining brand recognition, achieve a degree of control over their product that they could not achieve by depending on acquiring, promoting, and maintaining a stable of popular players, and they could do it more cheaply.

Biograph tried, longer than any other company, to install a system of product differentiation much in keeping with other forms of industrial production of the day. According to this scheme, "Biograph" would have the same kind of status that "Ford" and "Coca-Cola" were coming to have. However, although film, as a business, was to take up certain industrial practices, the dominant institutional pressures were to link film as symbolic act with traditional forms of artistic production. And of course these forms were heavily dependent on ideas of authorship. Art was, according to the romantic tenets of the day, an arena of individual expression. Biograph was certainly involved in associating film with this artistic tradition, but it wanted to exploit the advantages of this association while avoiding the perceived disadvantages of naming individuals' names. All of the companies undoubtedly faced the same problems as Biograph. However, it must be stressed that Biograph was the only company that pursued a policy of withholding players names after the initial explosion of publicity about picture personalities began.[71]

The acknowledgment of human labor as the source of moving pictures did not automatically bring about the recognition of actors. Other humans were involved in making films, so the attention given the actor was not uncontested. The "Picture Personality" section of *Moving Picture World* that included articles on Lepanto and Turner in 1909 and 1910 also included articles on such people as Chester Freeman, "erstwhile controlling spirit of the Film Import and Trading Company." An inventor also appeared as a picture personality;

the article stated, "The many users of the Nicholas Power machine might like to know something about the personality of the man whose name this beautiful piece of mechanism bears."[72] And Biograph, when it did finally announce that it would begin to acknowledge the names of the talent behind its pictures, announced that it would single out only camera operators and producers such as Dell Henderson, Tony O'Sullivan, and D. W. Griffith. Photoplaywrights were also given a great deal of attention in the publicity of a number of companies. As is still the case today, the actor's activity was held in a particular economy with other institutionally circumscribed enunciative activities. The efforts to turn the public attention toward Freeman, Henderson, O'Sullivan, or even Griffith were not wholly successful, however. The actor quickly became, for the public, the principal figure in the enunciative apparatus.

A third explanation for the concealment of the players' names was prevalent during the period. There was a fear that if the actors were known in real life it would spoil the illusion of the cinema. In a sense, this reasoning harks back to earlier discourses that attempted to locate textual productivity in the magic of the apparatus. We see a clear example of this in the 1907 article "The Cinematographer and Some of His Difficulties": "There were some things that the moving picture man would not reveal, but merely skimmed over with wise nods of the head and vague hints, because he believes too great a knowledge might rob the spectators of some of its keenness."[73] This reasoning is, in effect, an attempt to disavow or conceal the role of human labor in the production of film. What is odd though, is that it is still offered years after the involvement of human labor in production had become the central obsession of the public. In 1914, for instance, the Imp players appeared in person at the Republic Theater and spoke their lines as the film in which they starred was screened. Robert Grau, in *Theatre of Science,* reacted to this experiment in the following manner:

What can have possessed so intelligent a producer as Carl Laemmle to reveal to the general public "how motion pictures are made" is something few persons interested in the future of the new art can comprehend. . . . [W]hile un-doubtedly providing a novel entertainment, [it] seemed to merely emphasize the fact that, after all, the maze of scientific phenomena over which millions of fans were mystified was merely the work of ordinary humans and simple mechanics. If the gentlemen who have been enriched through the remarkable growth of a God-given art wish to put to a test the public's loyalty, let them continue to reveal the secrets of the film studio. Even now, the majority of film patrons know what never should have been discovered, namely, that the pictures are not taken consecutively. A year ago 95% of the public which patronizes the nickel and dime theatres were kept in suspense by their ignorance of the very things revealed through "The Baited Trap" production, and as to what percentage of these millions of new theatre-goers hold the illusion that photoplayers are superhuman or at least not merely human may quickly be learned if the country is flooded with such productions as "The Baited Trap."[74]

There is little evidence to support the claim that a knowledge of the actors spoiled the cinematic illusion. The fact that this was offered as an excuse for concealing information about the players reveals a great deal about the strategical functioning of discourse about this concealment, however. In bemoaning the public's knowledge of film production, Grau offers some clues to the specific articulation of power, knowledge, and pleasure that resulted in the sudden ascendancy of the picture personality after 1909. Grau's argument implies that the growth of the cinema between 1909 and 1915 was to some degree contingent upon the concealment of knowledge concerning the involvement of human labor in film production and the mystification this made possible. Although a work of concealment is constantly being pointed to, what is more evident during this same period is the intense proliferation of discourse about the involvement of human labor, an obsession with it that focused on the picture personality.

This seemingly contradictory situation is in many ways reminiscent of that discussed by Foucault in *The History of Sexuality*. Foucault argues that during the last three centuries sexuality has not been repressed, but rather there has been a veritable "discursive explosion" concerning it. "What is peculiar to modern societies, in fact, is not that they consigned sex to a shadow existence, but that they dedicated themselves to speaking of it *ad infinitum* as *the* secret."[75] The truth of the human labor involved in film was constituted similarly as a secret, one whose discovery would be all the more precious and pleasurable since it would emerge out of ostensible attempts to conceal it. The picture personality became the site of this truth and consequently, the biggest secret of all. This truth was figured at first as a very simple question of identity—a name. If the moviegoer did not know the names of particular players there was an explanation for his or her ignorance available: those players' names could not be revealed because the players were, in fact, well-known legitimate actors. Such an explanation hardly resolves the enigma, however; it only compounds it, doubling its status as secret.

The name was not the only aspect of the picture personality that was constituted as a secret, though it is one of the most basic and has been singled out most intently by previous histories. Grau's reaction to *The Baited Trap* reveals the secretive context within which all knowledge of the photoplayer's work in film emerged. There is little doubt that the general public already knew "the very things revealed through *The Baited Trap* production" (That the picture personalities were real people? That they could appear in the theater and on the screen at the same time?). Nevertheless, the sentiments voiced by Grau fulfilled a discursive function. By stating the importance of keeping that knowledge from the public he continued to reproduce its status as secret.

A large percentage of the early discourse on picture personalities presented itself as explicitly posing or revealing a secret. The Marion Leonard promotion, for instance, was heavily dependent on this strategy. The "Twinkle, Twinkle, Little Star" poem is a clear example of this. But clearer still is the following passage from an article in *Moving Picture News* entitled "So I Went to See Marion Leonard":

For weeks there had been whisperings and wondering regarding the gifted lady's absence from the screen; rumors and reasons ran riot; conjectures and questions followed fast and followed faster; but the oracle was mute, and there was none who knew the answer. The perplexing puzzle lingered and lengthened. Exhibitors asked, and a question was their answer. Exchange men inquired, and learned only a mystery. Manufacturers furrowed their brows—and that wasn't the only plowing they did. But the elusive and illusive Miss Leonard became more so. Until—.[76]

An article in *Moving Picture World* displays this same fascination with secrecy, though it gives it a fairly anticlimactic twist. "After this caption ["Mignon Anderson—Her Secret"] many will expect to read something thrilling about the popular Thanhouser player, but the *World* will clear the air by saying that the only connection between Miss Anderson and "Her Secret" is that her latest appearance is in a film of that name."[77] Note the following lines from an interview in *The Motion Picture Story Magazine* with Whitney Raymond. It is a fairly typical celebrity interview, and yet the secretive nature of the information revealed is emphasized by setting it up not as a celebrity interview but as an overheard conversation:

I hadn't the least idea that the editor would permit me, a mere fan, to interview my favorite, but, to my surprise and delight, he did, and I quickly made my way to the home of Whitney Raymond. The maid ushered me into the library and politely asked me to wait a minute—she would summon Mr. Raymond directly. A minute! I admired the endless rows of leather-bound volumes and reflected that Mr. Raymond must be fond of reading. Then I sat tapping the floor and chewing on my pencil—for an age, it seemed, before I heard footfalls down the hall. I straightened my hat and called forth my pleasantest smile, only to be disappointed. The footsteps passed the door and entered the room adjoining. "Hello, Harry, old boy!" a pleasant voice greeted warmly. "This *is* a treat after so many years." And I knew instinctively

that the speaker was the man I had been detailed to "chat." I
didn't want to eavesdrop, but it wasn't my fault that the door
was open a crack, and that the maid had been negligent. I
clutched my pencil tightly. Anything I learned now would be
real news and not just the modest information I would have
been able to extract.

The writer recounts part of a conversation in which Raymond man-
ages to work in just the sort of "modest information" typical of such
an interview. Then he writes, "I was wishing 'Harry' [Raymond]
would speak louder. This was really interesting—particularly the part
I can't put down here—tho all the time I knew it wasn't just."[78]
Information is not merely being provided about the photoplayers
here; secrets are being displayed and, to a degree, divulged. In these
examples we see this quite explicitly. However, the point I am making here is that all knowledge produced about the photoplayers carried with it connotations of secrecy. A kind of hermeneutic structure
subtended the reception of film, one that led the spectator from an
illusion presented in film through a series of questions to a "reality"
behind it. The spectators' sense that they were uncovering secrets
with every answer gleaned from the films and fan magazines piqued
their will to knowledge and afforded a bonus of pleasure with every
"discovery."

Having said this, we can conclude by returning to the problem of
the concealment of the players' names. There probably was some
resistance to the revelation of the players names. There were probably some actors who were embarrassed by the idea of publicity because they felt that they were just moonlighting to achieve their more
lofty goals. And the manufacturers must have realized that publicity
would result in higher wage demands by star performers. The point to
be made, however, is that these resistances (which were not, in any
case, equal to the various opposing pressures) were not an impedi-
ment to the emergence of the star system after 1909. Quite the
contrary—the sense that information about the players was being
held back was an integral, and often quite consciously utilized, part
of the publicity efforts designed to promote personalities. Real resis-

tances fit as well into the veil of secrecy that defined the picture personality as those that were fabricated. Both worked to solicit the public's will to knowledge.

The questions in the fan magazines about the names of the actors who appeared in particular films point to the difficulty of separating the circulation of the players' names from the circulation of the films they were in. What is at issue here is a type of identification in the most usual sense of the word: the identification of an actor in a specific film with a name. However, this identification extended well beyond the single film. What the name designated above all was a form of intertextuality, the recognition and identification of an actor from film to film. This intertextuality emerged as a measure of the increasing regularity and regulation of the cinematic institution—both in its product (the same actors appeared regularly) and, more crucially perhaps, in its audience, which had to go to the cinema often for this intertextual meaning to arise. The second aspect of the picture personalities' existence in discourse is in a strictly delineated field of intertextuality that I have termed the "image." The player's name was both the designation of and the support for the image, so the two are obviously intricately related. But they are not coextensive. It is necessary then to ascertain what could be known about the player other than his or her name.

The image was, first of all, a physical image, one that circulated through films and then, as the publicity apparatus began to take shape, through photos in magazines, newspapers, postcards, and song slides. The recognition of a specific actor's image was, as we have noted, basic to the emergence of the picture personality. There are a number of interesting questions about the purely visual identity of the actor that cannot be fully addressed here—how it related to broad cultural notions of beauty and sexuality; how, once constituted, this identity could become self-reflexively put into play within the film (through various strategies of dissimulation—makeup, costuming, etc.).

Another aspect of the image, one we will be much more concerned with here, extends beyond the physical appearance of the actor into the realm of what was called personality. It corresponds very roughly to what we speak of when we speak of a star's image. Yet the "personality" in this case was defined along a much more narrow range of coordinates. As the term *picture personality* indicates, the site of interest was the personality of the player as represented on film. There was thus a kind of restriction of knowledge about the players to the textuality of the films they were in, one that was supported, as we shall see, in extrafilmic discourse as well.

A 1910 article from *Moving Picture World* points clearly to the way in which the personalities of the players were apprehended: "Quite recently a well-known lady writing us in regard to her liking for the picture, used the phrase: she was so used to the personalities of the players, that she felt as though she actually knew them. This we believe voices a common feeling."[79] The player's personality was to be gleaned, first and foremost, from the films themselves. The magazines of the period perpetuated the association in their descriptions of actors: Mary Pickford has "a vigorous, winning personality that pervades her work"; Mabelle Trunelle's personality "stood out prominently" in her first picture; Helen Gardner's "beautiful personality" will "saturate" her new films.[80] A fan sent the following poem into *The Motion Picture Story Magazine:*

> There is one whose personality
> Is strong—so strong it seems
> That it haunts me with its power
> Awake and in night's dreams
> The strong magnetic noble face
> The firmly moulded chin
> The eyes, so dark and honest
> Show the character within.[81]

Personality existed as an effect of the representation of character in a film—or, more accurately, as the effect of the representation of character across a number of films. It functioned primarily to ascribe a unity to the actor's various appearances in films. However, although personality was primarily an effect of the representation of character within films, the illusion that it had its basis outside the film was constantly maintained. When we are told that Mary Pickford's personality "pervades" her work we are to assume that that personality exists independent of her work but that through her talent she can express it on film. This assumption upholds the play of surface and depth, inside and outside, that is the basis of the hermeneutic described earlier and that in fact characterizes all discourse on the picture personality. The spectator is led from the fiction and the characters that inhabit it to a supposed reality, truth, and origin behind it—the player's personality. This emphasis on the exteriority of the picture personality is clear in a section of *Photoplay* that in July 1913 was retitled "Photoplayers' Personalities: Little Glimpses behind the Screen as It Were."[82]

The glimpses behind the screen might as well have been glimpses of the screen though. Extrafilmic discourse did talk about the players' personalities outside of films but only to claim that they were the same as those represented in films. This is the most important point to be made about the knowledge produced about the picture personality, and it is what I mean when I say that the player's identity was restricted to the textuality of the films she or he was in. Even the articles that promised to reveal what the players were really like merely reproduced the representations of personality already produced in films. Differences between actor and character were to a large degree disavowed.[83] A few examples should make this clearer. For instance, note the way in which the similarities between Baggot and his current role are stressed in the following passage: "It was indeed a kingly occasion when I met Mr. King Baggot, of the 'King Edward'—kingly in more than mere name, for his bearing is regal, his manner royal, his actions princely. By which I mean that he is young (not too much so), dignified (just enough so), and gallant (oh, most so!). In a word, he is hero-esque."[84] In another context we are assured that King Baggot is "just as good a fellow off stage as on." Florence Turner is said to be "much the same out of a picture as she is in one." And Edna Fischer, because she worked with a broken ankle, was, just as she was in films, "a real heroine."[85]

All of these lines point to the way discourse about the player's existence outside of films emerged merely as an extension of an existence already laid out within films. The illusion that was operative was that the player's real personality (as presented in magazines) preceded and caused the representation of personality on the screen. In finding out about the players' personalities, spectators supposed they were learning something about the real conditions of the film's enunciation. But actually the represented "real" personalities were not primary; they were reduplications of a more basic representation of character within films. One of the defining features of discourse about picture personalities is a kind of redundancy, one that stretches across such central oppositions as surface and depth, illusion and reality, and enounced and enunciation. The regulation of knowledge effected through this redundancy is clear: everything written about the players' real personalities would support, amplify, and, in effect, advertise, the representations for sale in the movies themselves.

The following statements are fairly typical journalistic presentations of picture personalities:

> Miss Clara Williams is one of the most popular players. While she has had fine success in other roles, she excels in plays of the West. Having spent several years on a cattle ranch, she is familiar with the real cowboy. She is an expert horsewoman and a lover of outdoor life. All of Miss Williams's impersonations are highly artistic.

> Frank Lanning is of Irish extraction but when seen in Indian regalia it is difficult to distinguish him from the real article. In fact his strong features and strong build are so characteristic of the Indian race that he needs no disguise. [86]

In both passages the stress is laid on the similarities between the "real" actor and his or her roles. In Lanning's case the two are almost indistinguishable. It is the physical image that is referred to here, but if personality had been mentioned, the same kind of match would have undoubtedly been described. In fact, when Lanning was asked to explain his success in acting he replied, "one cannot express more than one really is."[87] A more apt formulation would have been "one is no more than one expresses on film," for this defines fairly accurately the tautological existence of the picture personality.

This existence found its quintessential expression in the series and serials popular during the period. Since the actor appeared explicitly as the same character in film after film, his or her appearances were unified by a consistent set of personality traits. Moreover, it is evident that the personality thus constituted, the character's identity, was conflated with the identity of the actor. In fact, the leading characters in the serials usually bore the same first name as the actors playing them. Thus, King Baggot played King the detective in the Imp detective series. Kathlyn Williams played the lead in *The Adventures of Kathlyn*.[88] Mary Pickford, though her films with Imp were called the "Little Mary Series," never appeared explicitly as the same character from film to film, yet her early work takes on many of the qualities of the series. For instance, the first Majestic release, *The Courting of Mary*, was about a relationship that developed between Mary (played by Pickford) and Owen (played by Owen Moore). Everything about this practice of naming characters after actors served to diffuse the boundaries between the two and encourage one to take the personality of one for the other.

The series is a particularly strong example of the discourse that worked to produce the picture personality because the same character with the same personality appeared repeatedly in film after film. However, I would argue that most of the films of the period worked according to the same principle. Pickford may not have appeared as the orphaned, sixteen-year-old niece of John Manor in films before or after *The Courting of Mary*, but there were nevertheless a more general set of character traits she represented from film to film: virtue, innocence, exuberance, pride, etc. The narratives in the films of the period hinged on idealized representations of masculinity and femininity. Since the leading actors of the companies were cast regularly in these types of roles, it is not surprising that they themselves became idealized as their reality became established in discourse.[89] They were, after all, just like the characters they played, but, unlike those characters, they were real. The writer of the following lines grappled (at a fairly early date) with the contradiction between the insubstantiality of the actor's image on the screen and the spectator's tendency to fall in love with this image as if it were really human. The "substance" given as the resolution to this contradiction is, precisely, personality:

> "Matinee" and "johnnie" idols are very common stage attractions to a certain species of genus homo who frequent the theatre: the moving picture gods and goddesses are of recent discovery. We can understand how a person can "fall in love" with the living and attractive presence of an actor or actress, but it is incomprehensible how men and women will "fall in love" with moving picture actors as seen on screen, yet it is a fact attested and established by the number of requests and letters we receive from persons inquiring the names of and soliciting introductions to Vitagraph leading men and women. It proves that the acting as well as their personalities must be pretty much the real thing.

A third and final aspect of the discourse that produced the picture personality pertained to the professional experience of the actor. The actor's previous film experience worked to establish intertextual connections between films. For example, note this description of Dorothy Phillips: "Miss Dorothy Phillips—Played engenue leads with the Essanay Eastern stock company. Played Ruth in 'The Rosary,' or 'The Two Devotions' and Mary in 'Her Dad, the Constable.' Watch for her in the following Essanay photoplays soon to appear: 'The New Manager,' 'Love in the Hills,' 'The Gordian Knot,' etc."[90] The function of this kind of information is clear: to establish the actor's identity across a number of films.

These credentials were not restricted to film appearances, however. Most writing about picture personalities touted the actor's past theatrical experience as well, and, by doing so, continued the discourse on acting:

> Miss Grace Cunard—From footlights to film is the way the stories of most photoplayers run these days. Grace Cunard, heroine of the Republic subject, "Before Yorktown," is no exception, for her theatrical career dates back almost as far

as she can remember, when at the age of fifteen she played leading juvenile parts in stock. She has since appeared with different companies, starring in "College Days" during the season of 1910.

Francis Xavier Bushman—Playing leading roles in Essanay photoplays. In recent photoplays appeared in "Her Dad, the Constable," "God's Inn by the Sea," "The New Manager," etc. Mr. Bushman's theatrical career began sixteen years ago and has been associated with a number of the leading stock companies in the principal cities of the country. Mr. Bushman is an exceptionally fine picture subject and a talented actor. [91]

At one level, such statements are obviously aimed at establishing the artistic authority of individual actors. Yet, as one reads similar statements about actor after actor, one realizes that they function in terms of a broader strategy—to legitimize film acting in general by associating it with the acting of the legitimate stage. The claim that Cunard and Bushman and the dozens of others appearing in films had merely transferred their talents from stage to screen was an elegant way of accomplishing this.

What is most surprising about the discourse that emerged to produce the picture personality is that although it supposedly addressed an intense interest in everything about the actors appearing in films, it revealed very little about them. In fact, many of the aspects of the actor's existence that we find most compelling today were never systematically addressed during the years prior to 1913. There were very real limits to what could be said and what could be known about the picture personalities. Their identity was almost wholly a product of their appearances in films. Extrafilmic discourse insisted on the personality's real-world identity, to be sure, but in describing that identity it merely referred readers back to the evidence of the films in a kind of tautological loop.

Because of this, the information provided about the picture personalities in fan magazines and newspapers usually seems quite meager:

Warren Kerrigan—He has gathered quite a following of admirers among the moving picture theatre audiences, and his splendid work is so well known to the average moving picture patron that nothing we say will enhance the impression that he has already made in the moving picture field with his handsome appearance and clever and versatile acting.

King Baggot certainly needs no introduction to picture "fans" for he is easily one of the most popular of the male stars. Handsome in every sense of the word and possessing a wonderful ability to "put over" a big scene, Mr. Baggot is naturally called upon to enact most of the leading roles in IMP productions. So popular has he become that it is only necessary for exhibitors to announce "King Baggot appears today," in order to pack their theaters at every performance.[92]

The main function of this information is merely to acknowledge an identity constituted elsewhere. Even though the player's "real life" identity was delineated, it was drawn from his or her appearance in films. It was, in short, a professional existence—a history of appearances in films and plays and a personality gleaned from those appearances.

NOTES

1. *Sunday Magazine, St. Louis Post-Dispatch*, Mar. 20, 1910, p. 1.
2. *New York Dramatic Mirror*, Jan. 2, 1909, p. 6.
3. *Moving Picture World*, Jan. 15, 1910, p. 50.
4. See, for instance, *The Edison Kinetogram*, Sept. 1, 1909, p. 3, which includes cast lists for *Ethel's Luncheon* and *Little Sister*.
5. Ibid., Oct. 15, 1909, p. 3.
6. Ibid., Oct. 1, 1909, p. 3, and Dec. 15, 1909, p. 1; *Moving Picture World*, Nov. 13, 1909, p. 682.
7. *Moving Picture World*, Feb. 26, 1910, p. 294.
8. Ibid.
9. Letter from John H. Fin, Jr., to the American Biograph Company,

Dec. 17, 1908. All letters referred to here are from the Florence Lawrence Collection at the Los Angeles County Museum of Natural History.

10. Alexander Walker, *Stardom: The Hollywood Phenomenon* (New York: Stein and Day, 1970), pp. 19–39; Letter to Florence Lawrence from mother, Aug. 9, 1910.

11. *Moving Picture World*, Mar. 29, 1909, p. 740; *Sunday Magazine, St. Louis Post-Dispatch*, Mar. 20, 1910, p. 4. Such figures were, of course, frequently exaggerated. This salary corresponds to that which Lawrence later received at Lubin, so it may be accurate. It seems doubtful, though, that Lawrence was to receive this salary for life.

12. *Moving Picture World*, Dec. 18, 1909, p. 866.

13. Letter from Sarah Bendall to Lawrence, Nov. 6, 1909.

14. Letter from Leland Ayers to Lawrence, Dec. 27, 1909.

15. Letter from May Woelfil to Lawrence, Feb. 16, 1910.

16. *Moving Picture World*, Mar. 5, 1910, p. 365.

17. *Sunday Magazine, St. Louis Post-Dispatch*, Mar. 6, 1910, p. 4.

18. *Moving Picture World*, Mar. 19, 1910, p. 409.

19. *Sunday Magazine, St. Louis Post-Dispatch*, Mar. 20, 1910, p. 1.

20. *Moving Picture World*, Apr. 2, 1910, p. 517.

21. Letter from H. L. Salter to Lawrence, Aug. 1, 1910. See also the letter to Lawrence from her mother, July 10, 1910, in which she says, "How are matters progressing now with Cochrane and you. I do not believe in these fights."

22. Letter to Lawrence from brother Norman, Aug. 10, 1910; letter to Lawrence from mother, Aug. 9, 1910; passenger list, The American Line Steamship *Merion*, Sept. 10, 1910, in the Florence Lawrence Collection, Los Angeles County Museum of Natural History.

23. *Moving Picture World*, Oct. 22, 1910, p. 956.

24. Ibid., Nov. 14, 1911, p. 421; regarding the lawsuit see the letter to Lawrence from her brother Norman, Jan. 12, 1911; *Moving Picture World*, Dec. 24, 1910, p. 1462.

25. Letter to Lawrence from her brother Norman, Jan. 12, 1911; *Moving Picture World*, May 18, 1912, p. 617; Letter to Lawrence from her mother, June 11, 1912. An article in *Moving Picture World* announcing her return (May 18, 1912, p. 617) said that she had left because she needed mental rest. In the same issue it was announced that Florence Turner was returning to film work after a seven-month rest necessitated by overexhaustion.

26. *Moving Picture World*, May 18, 1912, p. 617.

27. Letters to Lawrence from her mother, May 24, 1912; June 18, 1912; and July 9, 1912.

28. Letter to Lawrence from her mother, July 9, 1912.

29. *Moving Picture News*, Aug. 2, 1913, p. 15.

30. *Moving Picture World*, Sept. 13, 1913, p. 1242.

31. *Photoplay*, July 1913, p. 61; *Motion Picture Story*, Oct. 1913, p. 109.

32. *Moving Picture World*, Apr. 2, 1910, p. 515; July 23, 1910, p. 187.

33. Ibid., July 23, 1910, p. 187. *Stage* here refers to the Vitagraph stage, that is, moving pictures.

34. Ibid., Apr. 23, 1910, p. 644.

35. Ibid., July 9, 1910, p. 114.

36. Ibid., Dec. 31, 1910, p. 1521.

37. Ibid., Jan. 14, 1911, p. 73.

38. Epes Winthrop Sargent, "Advertising for Exhibitors," *Moving Picture World*, Oct. 21, 1911, p. 195.

39. *Moving Picture World*, May 18, 1912, p. 622; Mar. 22, 1913, p. 1225; *Moving Picture News*, Dec. 13, 1913, p. 12, and Dec. 6, 1913, p. 51; Anthony Slide, *The Big V: A History of the Vitagraph Company* (Metuchen, N.J.: Scarecrow Press, 1976), pp. 34–40.

40. *Moving Picture World*, Oct. 1, 1910, p. 726; see also, Ibid., Oct. 8, 1910, p. 848.

41. *Moving Picture News*, Nov. 11, 1911, p. 13, and *Moving Picture World*, Nov. 18, 1911, p. 539.

42. *Moving Picture News*, Nov. 18, 1911, p. 9.

43. Ibid., Nov. 25, 1911, p. 9, and *Moving Picture World*, Dec. 2, 1911, p. 737.

44. *Moving Picture News*, Dec. 9, 1911, p. 7, and Dec. 30, 1911, pp. 24–25; *Moving Picture World*, Jan. 20, 1912, p. 269.

45. *Moving Picture News*, Feb. 17, 1912, p. 14.

46. *Moving Picture World*, Feb. 24, 1912, p. 672; *Moving Picture News*, June 18, 1912, p. 21.

47. *Moving Picture World*, Dec. 24, 1910, p. 1462.

48. Ibid., Jan. 7, 1911, p. 4; Jan. 28, 1911, p. 168; Feb. 11, 1911, pp. 280, 323; Jan. 14, 1911, p. 60.

49. Ibid., Oct. 21, 1911, p. 27; *New York Times*, Oct. 15, 1911, pt. 3, p. 10; *Moving Picture News*, Oct. 28, 1911, p. 3, and *Moving Picture World*, Nov. 4, 1911, p. 345.

50. *Moving Picture World*, Feb. 8, 1913, p. 585.

51. Ibid., May 17, 1913, p. 707.

52. See for instance an article in *Moving Picture World* entitled "Miss Pickford at Her Best," Nov. 15, 1913, p. 718; *Photoplay*, Aug. 1913, pp. 34–35, and *Motography*, Aug. 23, 1913, pp. 125–26; *Moving Picture World*, Nov. 29, 1913, p. 1015.

53. *Moving Picture World*, Dec. 17, 1910, p. 1402.

54. *Motion Picture Story*, Feb. 1911, p. 111; *Moving Picture World*, Oct. 7, 1911, p. 9.

55. Ibid., Aug. 5, 1911, p. 309; May 24, 1913, p. 816; Aug. 12, 1911, p. 379; *Motography*, Apr. 1911, cover.

56. Anthony Slide, *Aspects of American Film History Prior to 1920* (Metuchen, N.J.: Scarecrow Press, 1978), pp. 1–2.

57. See Roland Barthes, *S/Z*, trans. Richard Howard (New York: Hill and Wang, 1974).

58. *Motion Picture Story*, Nov. 1912, p. 125; July 1913, p. 127.

59. Ibid., Nov. 1912, p. 135; Oct. 1913, p. 109.

60. There were in fact at least two such contests held by this magazine during this period, one announced in January 1912 and another announced in November 1912. The top five actors in the latter contest were Romaine Fielding, Earle Williams, Warren Kerrigan, Alice Joyce, and Carlyle Blackwell. See *Motion Picture Story*, Jan. 1912, p. 144; Nov. 1912, p. 144; and Oct. 1913, p. 109. One has to wonder what the relationship was between voting in these contests and the suffrage movement that was under way at this time.

61. *Photoplay* had regular contests during this time as well. In July 1913 the results of one of these were announced. The top five winners were Warren Kerrigan, Marguerite Snow, James Cruze, King Baggot, and Florence Lawrence. See *Photoplay*, Mar. 1912, p. 70; July 1913, p. 61; and Sept. 1913, p. 74. In *The Ladies World* contest the readers' votes determined which of the seven following actors would appear in the film *One Wonderful Night*: King Baggot, Maurice Costello, Crane Wilbur, Arthur Johnson, Carlyle Blackwell, Francis Bushman, or Warren Kerrigan. Bushman won.

62. *Photoplay*, May 1912, p. 86; *Motion Picture Story*, Jan. 1912, p. 135.

63. *Moving Picture World*, Nov. 13, 1909, p. 682.

64. Ibid., Nov. 12, 1910, p. 1099.

65. Ibid., July 29, 1911, p. 216.

66. William H. Kitchell, "The Artists of the Screen," *Moving Picture World*, Sept. 30, 1911, p. 949; *Photoplay*, Nov. 1912, p. 110; *Motion Picture*

Story, Nov. 1913, p. 105. There is also the question raised here of where the credits should go—at the beginning, at the end, or in installments as the characters are introduced (the latter had been an innovation of the Edison Company).

67. Slide, *Aspects of American Film History*, p. 3. The "proof" behind the argument that the actors might have damaged their careers was perhaps the fact that, according to Robert Grau in *The Theatre of Science*, some noted Broadway actors who had made forays into vaudeville had indeed damaged their careers.

68. *Moving Picture World*, Dec. 23, 1911, p. 971.

69. Frank E. Woods, "Why Is a Star?" *Photoplay*, Nov. 1919, p. 70.

70. *Moving Picture World*, Mar. 22, 1913, p. 1207.

71. Biograph's abandonment to its policy was gradual and can be briefly traced here. An article in *Moving Picture World* on March 22, 1911, announced "Biograph Players May Be Known." "Current gossip here is to the effect that within a few weeks the public will be informed that there are actually human beings connected with the Biograph Company and that the figures which the patrons of motion picture theaters have seen on the screen when Biographs were being run are men and women, who have names and identities—talents" (p. 1207). However, the indication was that the change in policy at this point concerned only the names of producers and camera operators. Griffith's rise to fame is interesting in this regard, and indeed, he is mentioned in the article. In early 1912, *Motion Picture Story's* "Answers to Inquiries" feature was still not answering questions about the Biograph players, explaining that they have "no official identity" (Jan. 1912, p. 134). No Biograph player placed among the thirty-three top players announced in the *Photoplay* "Great Popularity Contest of July 1913" (July 1913, p. 61). Two Biograph players placed in *Motion Picture Story's* October contest (Blanche Sweet, twenty-first, and Gertrude Robinson, forty-seventh). However, the top one hundred recipients of votes were noted. Vitagraph, by contrast, placed eighteen players and Thanhouser seven. It was not until early 1914 that one sees strong evidence of player promotion on the part of Biograph. In January 1914, Blanche Sweet was featured in *Motion Picture Story*, and the next month the magazine's answer department was full of identifications of Biograph actors (Jan. 1914, p. 99, and Feb. 1914, p. 115).

72. *Moving Picture World*, May 21, 1910, p. 823; May 14, 1910, p. 776.

73. Ibid., July 13, 1907, p. 298.

74. Robert Grau, *Theatre of Science* (New York: Broadway, 1914), p. 146.

75. Michel Foucault, *The History of Sexuality*, vol. 1, trans. Robert Hurley (New York: Pantheon Books, 1978), p. 35.

76. *Moving Picture News*, Dec. 9, 1911, p. 7.

77. *Moving Picture World*, June 8, 1912, p. 921.

78. *Motion Picture Story*, Sept. 1913, p. 122.

79. *Moving Picture World*, Nov. 12, 1910, p. 1099.

80. Ibid., Dec. 24, 1910, p. 1492; Sept. 24, 1910, p. 680; June 8, 1912, p. 998.

81. *Motion Picture Story*, July 1913, p. 117.

82. It had previously been titled "Notes on the Players." See *Photoplay*, July 1913, p. 79.

83. It should be noted however that it was necessary to mark a difference between these two when making certain claims about acting, since the actor's skill was displayed most by the variety of roles she or he could play. The article on Turner (cited below) interestingly enough claims that "she is just as willing to play a slavey as she would to portray a king." But then it goes on to say she is the same on-screen and off-screen. One might legitimately ask whether she is more like a slave or a king in real life. What we see here is a contradiction between the regulation of knowledge characteristic of the picture personality and the requirements of the discourse on acting.

84. *Motion Picture Story*, Nov. 1912, p. 130.

85. *Moving Picture World*, Feb. 3, 1912, p. 409; May 18, 1912, p. 622; Dec. 16, 1911, p. 894.

86. *Motion Picture Story*, Feb. 1911, p. 13; *Moving Picture World*, Feb. 4, 1911, p. 245.

87. *Moving Picture World*, Feb. 4, 1911, p. 245.

88. *Moving Picture News*, Oct. 28, 1911, p. 28; Jan. 17, 1914, p. 38.

89. It is important to note, in this regard, that actors who played villains during these years did not become famous as picture personalities.

90. *Moving Picture World*, Mar. 26, 1910, p. 468; July 29, 1911, p. 231.

91. *Moving Picture World*, Dec. 23, 1911, p. 972; Aug. 5, 1911, p. 309.

92. *The Nickelodeon*, Jan. 7, 1911, p. 19; *Photoplay*, May 1912, p. 80.

The Star

In 1913 and 1914 one can begin to see a significant transformation in the regulation of knowledge concerning the player, one that brought into existence the star. The star emerged out of a marked expansion of the type of knowledge that could be produced about the player. The picture personality was defined, as we have seen, by a discourse that restricted knowledge to the professional existence of the actor. With the emergence of the star, the question of the player's existence outside his or her work in film became the primary focus of discourse. The private lives of the players were constituted as a site of knowledge and truth.

As an article in 1916 noted, "There are several questions agitating the Great American Public. . . . But one of the most important of these questions comes from the family of fans . . . and that question is, 'What do they [the players] do when they're not working?'"[1] A passage from a short story of the same year, "The Glory Road," offers perhaps the best illustration of the kind of interest that would characterize the star:

> In the studios—behind the "movie" screen—what a mystery-land lies there! Those within may close and bolt the door, but they cannot keep the lure of it from seeping through. The life that artists live beats often with a more feverish pulse than the lives their art depicts. Its passions, its strivings and defeats, its pay and—its price; what a writhing and a weaving in and out we should peer at, if only the door were

not shut! What a tumult worth watching! A world of art, of itself and sufficient to itself.[2]

The revelations about this "mysteryland" were made in a secretive context just as all of the previous revelations about the actors' identities. And yet the content of the secret was different here, because it had very little, if anything, to do with the actor's appearance in films. With the star the actor became a character in a narrative quite separable from his or her work in any film.

Serialized stories about moving picture life (such as "The Glory Road") appeared regularly throughout the teens and twenties and are perhaps the best evidence of the type of narrative that produced the star. "My Experiences as a Film Favorite" and "Loree Starr—Photoplay Idol" are the earliest of these stories, and, in my mind, the clearest indication of the shift that took place in 1913 and 1914.

"My Experiences as a Film Favorite" was billed as "An Intensely Interesting and Intimate Inside Story of Moving Picture Life as Related by a Well-known Photoplay Actress."[3] Polly Dean (a pseudonym—the actress's real name could not be revealed) was a small-town girl who moved to New York to find success on the stage. After several attempts to get a chance on the stage failed, she got a job in a film company through the influence of its leading man, Paul Poinsaire, with whom she had fallen in love. Poinsaire's intentions were not honorable, however. After wining and dining Polly he asked her to become his mistress. When she refused he had her discharged from the company. Polly managed to get a job with another company, Excelsior (in the story one of the first of the Independents), and she was put under the direction of John Burton, a man whose exacting nature was easily mistaken for cruelty. Polly hated Burton at first, though he soon began to turn her into an excellent actress. Burton, for his part, had little respect for Polly because he thought she had been hired by the manager of the company in return for sexual favors. All of this changed one night when the manager tried to rape Polly and Burton saved her at the last minute. They both realized that they had misjudged each other and began to fall in love. The manager immediately fired both of them. When Burton was offered a job as the principal director of a new company on the west coast he included Polly in the deal. She arrived on the set the first day to discover that the male star of the company was Paul Poinsaire. She was content to conduct everything on a businesslike basis. Yet Poinsaire, fascinated by her aloofness, fell in love with her and asked her to marry him. She refused: " 'If you were the only man on earth to marry, and I had to marry you or beg in the streets—I'd beg!' "[4] Poinsaire tried to get Burton to fire Polly, but he refused and Poinsaire left the company. Burton rewrote the film the company was working on to feature Polly as the sole star. Its success assured Polly's destiny as an internationally famous movie star. And, at the end of the story, she married the man she loved, John Burton.

"My Experiences as a Film Favorite" combines many of the conventional narrative elements of the day: an Algeresque success story, a melodramatic opposition between country and city, and a last-minute rescue of the female and her virtue (reminiscent of Griffith's *The Lonely Villa*). What is remarkable about this story is that it presents film actors as the leading characters of such a narrative. This permitted an elaboration of the actor's identity far beyond that which had been possible earlier. The actor's "real" identity was no longer merely a shadowy extension of his or her work in film; it was much more—something that could emerge out of a richly drawn and relatively autonomous narrative.

"Loree Starr—Photoplay Idol" began its run in *Photoplay* in January 1914, three months after "My Experiences as a Film Favorite" began. There are at least two important differences between the two stories. First, "Loree Starr" was presented explicitly as a fiction whereas "My Experiences as a Film Favorite" was to be taken as a true account. Second, "Loree Starr" concerned the tribulations of a male actor rising in the film world. Otherwise, however, the two stories are strikingly similar. Loree Starr, a St. Louis youth, moved to New York to act in the theater. There he became involved in moving picture work and became very successful. Lois Richards, the wife of his director, soon showed "a decided partiality" for him, causing gossip and jealousy among the other members of the company. Loree, however, resisted her love. In retaliation, Lois told her husband that

Loree had been making unwanted advances toward her. Loree was immediately fired. He soon secured a job with another company, however, and fell in love with its female star. Months later, Lois, still obsessed with Loree, "trapped" him and got him to come up to her apartment. Lois's husband happened to catch them there together, and he assumed the worst. He threatened to break the scandal to the press unless Loree did the honorable thing and married his wife. Loree, however, returned the next day with his newfound love, announced that they were soon to be married, and got Lois to admit her deceitfulness. The problem was resolved.

The basic conventions of these stories obviously turn on alliances between the sexes within the closed world of studio life. Some of these alliances are motivated by manipulation and lechery, others by courtship and marriage. Virtuous alliances always triumph in the end. These alliances are above all else personal ones. Business relations—the power of the director over the actor or the actor over the extra—inevitably affect these alliances, yet the course the narrative follows privileges such things as struggles of conscience and the blossoming of love. It concerns itself obsessively with the private sphere—that which goes on "behind the doors" of the movie studios and "behind the screen" of the public spectacle.

The genre of Hollywood fiction, which has been examined in its novelistic form in detail by Carolyn See, actually began with these stories.[5] An expansion of the identity of the film actor was necessary for such fiction to be written, and, in fact, these particular stories had an important part in establishing the expanded identity of the star. The most remarkable aspect of "Loree Starr—Photoplay Idol" is perhaps its subtitle: "A Fascinating Serial Story Presenting a New Type of Hero." This hero is precisely the star as distinguished from the picture personality. Yet, it would be a mistake to imply that fictional discourse was the sole factor in the establishment of the star. During 1913 and 1914 there was a concomitant rise of journalistic discourse about the players that focused just as intently on their private lives. And this discourse undoubtedly solicited the public's interest and belief to a greater degree since it focused on the real players that could be seen and identified on the screen. In a very short period of time the journalistic apparatus that supported the star system became geared toward producing an endless stream of information about the private lives of the stars.

Stories about the private lives of theatrical actors had of course existed prior to the time a similar attention began to be focused on film actors. These stories had focused, through much of the nineteenth century, on the unconventional lifestyle of actors, on their rootlessness and moral laxity. Through these writings, "the actor" had attained the status of a character type with a standard set of (disreputable) traits and an expected manner of behavior.[6] When film actors became the subject of a similar "behind the scenes" type of narrative, their representation (and reception) was inevitably linked to the associations of this tradition. One of the principal strategies of the discourse that emerged to produce the movie star involved a kind of backlash against the theatrical model that in other ways, as we have seen, had been crucial in establishing the cinema's legitimacy. There is a consistent attempt in all of this writing to disassociate the film actor from the theatrical actor, to prove that the two were completely different from the standpoint of the conduct of their personal lives. The life of theatrical work was thus devalued as the life of film work was praised. Good examples of this occur throughout a series of articles in *Photoplay* entitled "Why Famous Film Favorites Forsook Footlights' Fascinations for Filmdom Fame." For instance, Harry S. Northrup explains his reasons for leaving the stage: "'What? The Stage? Not on your life, not if I know myself. Look around you here. What more could a man ask than this? A comfortable, attractive home, fifty-two weeks in the year income. Could the stage give me that? It could not.'"[7]

Theatrical comparisons concerning the private lives of the players were not welcome. The lives of theatrical stars had been quite commonly associated with scandals of all sorts. The discourse on the star involved a work that disassociated the film star from this aspect of the theatrical tradition. What was undoubtedly at stake here was reformist concern about the healthfulness of the cinema as an institution. The problem of public health was indeed one of the major expressions of resistance to the cinema.[8] Many of the theaters were presumably below accepted standards of cleanliness, and there were arguments that the cinema kept people from engaging in healthy, outdoor activity. The emphasis was not only on physical health, however; there was an equal concern about the moral healthfulness of the cinema. The discourse on the star worked to assert that the cinema was, "at its source," a healthy phenomenon. The truth revealed about the stars' private lives was, in fact, an image of pure health, one that was offered in stark contrast to the image of the theatrical star:

> Stage life, with its night work, its daytime sleep, its irregular meals, its travelling and close contact, does not make for a natural existence and throws a so-called glamor over many people. Contrast its possibilities with those of the picture studio. In the latter place work is done in regular office hours—daylight work; no glamor of night, of orchestra, of artificial light. A player is located in one neighborhood and is recognized as a permanent and respectable citizen. Evenings can be spent at home, and the normal healthiness of one's own fireside is an atmosphere conductive to refining influences. Healthy outdoor work and a permanent circle of friends make for a sane and not-precarious existence. The restlessness and loneliness of a life of travel is also eliminated. In the studios in which I have played there has always been a good fellowship, the camaraderie of a happy family. I hope that the general public will not be beguiled by any of the sensationalism or scandal regarding photoplayers which may be in circulation, but will recognize the movies as an industry which is as clean and wholesome at its source as it has proved itself entertaining and progressive at its outlet—to its audiences and patrons.
>
> Since the elevation of pictures to a higher level, a level which is comparable to the stage, manufacturers want actors and actresses of intelligence and refinement to depict their drawing room drama—supposed to reflect the higher strata of life. It is therefore hardly likely that they would engage

girls who would submit to such tests of immorality (as has been mentioned in a recent discussion), for such a character would show in their faces.[9]

As this passage indicates, the potential for scandal was both addressed and denied in early discourse on the star. This was equally evident in the serialized stories discussed earlier. Although Polly was exposed to the advances of depraved producers, she resisted them and maintained her reputation. Loree Starr, similarly, resisted sexual temptation and did what was morally correct. The film actor, as a character type, was to be a conventional hero or heroine in his or her personal narrative just as he or she was in films. The stage actor, in contrast, was associated with glamour. In fact, Harold Lockwood, praised for his "clean living and total abstinence," made the interesting claim that all of the evil elements in the moving picture field could be traced to the involvement of theater types: " 'In the near future,' " he philosophized, " 'this photoplay business, which is now in a more or less chaotic state because of the intermingling with people from the stage, is going to become stabilized. The unfit will be weeded out by the law of supply and demand.' "[10] So, the discourse on the stars' private lives worked to deny the applicability of previous characterizations of the actor and blunt the very real suspicions that there were immoral activities going on in "filmdom." Readers of *Photoplay* were told, for instance, that any society girl in their town or any other town was living "a life of scandalous dissipation" compared to Edna Mayo. George Holt, an infamous villain on the screen, terribly disappointed one writer when he proved to be in private life "an exemplary citizen."[11] And an article called "How Men and Women of the Motion Picture World Will Spend Their Christmas This Year" stressed the stability of film life by contrasting it to stage life: "To the profession, the players of the regular drama from Broadway to Skagway, Christmas Day is the time for remembrance that they are of a world apart. To the players of the motion picture world whose likenesses are entertaining more thousands of theater goers than ever packed into performances of the older drama Christmas

Day is a time for rejoicing that they may live like home folk."[12] Finally, along similar lines, a writer claimed that "the camera calling promotes domesticity because it provides a place of more or less permanent residence and invites home building. In pictures, the stage nomad is likely to become the town's pioneer resident."[13]

Most claims about the healthiness of the players' lives referred to this notion of domesticity and focused specifically on the family lives of the players. This was the most important aspect of "the private" as it was invoked to constitute the star. Nick Browne has argued that a family discourse underpinned the formation of early film narrative in the films of Griffith.[14] The emergence of the star marks the extension of this discourse into another sphere—one tied to the cinematic institution and the textuality of films but nevertheless outside of the film text narrowly defined. Just as the films were often about courtship and marriage, husbands and wives, parents and children, so was writing about the stars.

References to marriage and married life are ever present after 1913. There had admittedly been a few scattered references to photoplayers' marriages prior to this. In December 1911 *Moving Picture World* carried a short article on the marriage of two photoplayers who had been acting together, Mary Land and Howard Mitchell. At the end of the next year *Photoplay* briefly noted that Mary Pickford and Owen Moore were husband and wife.[15] The Marion Leonard promotion certainly played on curiosity about her marital status. A few other similar references could be noted, yet all these are exceptional instances and not significant in terms of the overall representation of the players. Much more than a quantitative shift took place in the early teens. The player's existence in discourse was substantially altered as the publicity apparatus became geared primarily toward the presentation of the love lives of the stars.

The kind of information provided in *Photoplay's* question and answer section demonstrates this shift quite vividly. "Answers to Inquiries" operated according to the following rules in 1912: "This department is for the answering of questions of general interest. Information as to matrimonial alliances and other purely personal matters will not be answered. Questions concerning the marriages of players will be completely ignored."[16] Within a short period of time, however, *Photoplay* would be providing answers such as the following:

> James Cruze, Marguerite Snow and Alice Joyce are married. Florence LaBadie, Mary Fuller and Charles Ogle are not.

> James Cruze and Marguerite Snow have one daughter, Julie, and she appeared in *The Million Dollar Mystery*.

> The report that Harold Lockwood and May Allison are married is untrue. Miss Allison says she has no time for such serious thoughts and Mr. Lockwood is understood to have been married in 1906.

By this point, the rules for the column read, "We ask only that questions regarding religion, scenario writing and studio employment be omitted."[17]

In February 1915 *Photoplay* initiated a series of articles entitled "Who's Married to Who in the Movies," which revealed which famous actors and actresses were married to each other. A later, similar feature was called "Who's Whose—When the Lamps Are Focused on the Dinner Tables instead of the Sets."[18] The *Motion Picture Story Magazine* (renamed the *Motion Picture Magazine* in 1915) did not begin contributing significantly to the expanding identity of the star until the middle teens. But in 1916 the interest quite explicitly shifted: "Perhaps everything has been written about Mary Pickford. All right then, let's hear about Mrs. Owen Moore. . . . Mrs. Moore is ever so much more beautiful than Mary Pickford."[19] In the fan magazines and in the trade press, readers learned about countless couples of the film world—Mr. and Mrs. Phillips Smalley, Mr. and Mrs. Herbert Prior, Allan Dwan and Pauline Bush, Joseph Roach and Ruth Stonehouse, Mr. and Mrs. Sydney Drew, Marc MacDermott and Miriam Nesbitt, and many others.[20] Articles identifying couples usually included the story of the couples' courtship or a treatise on their domestic bliss. Marital status inevitably came up in celebrity interviews and worked to figure the player's identity. A cartoon from 1919 illustrates, in an exaggerated way no doubt, just how this identity had entered into the reception of films. Two women enter a movie theater and, while watching the movie, spend so much time sorting out who the different actors are married to, they can't even tell a curious passerby who stops them after they leave the theater what movie they saw.[21]

The identification of couples was only one aspect of the family discourse that constituted the star, of course. There was also an emphasis on the players' children as well as their relationships with their mothers. In December 1916 there was a layout in *Photoplay* featuring pictures of popular players with their mothers. "You've got to give them credit," a caption read. It was often noted that actors, especially single actors, lived with their mothers.[22]

All of this worked to convince the public that film actors lived healthy, conventional lives behind the screen. Of course it was very difficult to separate the idea of family life from the idea of home life, so the stars' homes became another area of intense interest, another aspect of their private existence. In a January 1914 article, for instance, we learn about Helen Gardner's house—"a 'home' in every sense of the word," nestled "among pines and cedar," with a "large vegetable garden" and "many gables." "It is really a delightful place, and quite fit for its charming occupant. Here Miss Gardner and her mother, who looks no older than her daughter—and indeed, has one of those rare natures which never grow old—live happily, plan pictures, design costumes, and receive their friends."[23] Photo layouts of the houses of Mabel Normand, Phillips Smalley and Lois Weber, and Joseph Schenck and Norma Talmadge were among the many that appeared during these years.[24] The actors were shown reading or writing in their homes or posing proudly in front of them.

The connotations of conventionality, stability, and normalcy that could be attached to the presentation of the star's homes were important to the argument that film actors led healthy lives. Yet these connotations existed along with others that increasingly, no doubt, overshadowed them. In many respects the houses of the stars were obviously not normal. They were, in fact, immense, luxurious, and excessive. The discourse on the star took part in another strategy, one designed not so much to uphold traditional values of family and home as it was to promote the values of consumerism that began to dominate American life in the teens and twenties. Lary May, in *Screening Out the Past*, has described how the tensions between Victorian ideals and consumer ideals were worked out in shifts in film culture between 1908 and 1929.[25] Stars, he argues, were a privileged site for the promulgation and solidification of new consumer ideals. Their wealth could not be ascribed to the exploitation of the many by the few. On the contrary, since they had very little real social power (though very much status), and since most of them came from common backgrounds, their success was easily ascribed to democratic aspiration. In conspicuously displaying that success through material possessions, the star vividly demonstrated the idea that satisfaction was not to be found in work but in one's activities away from work—in consumption and leisure. Thus, much of the writing focused specifically on how the stars spent their enormous salaries and how they spent their leisure time. The emphasis on homes is not only an emphasis on family life, but also on the pleasures of wealth and leisure. This is clear in an article that presents a photo of a famous star outside of her house playing football and a caption that reads, "Where Norma Talmadge and her husband 'keep house'—as well as get their recreation." And *Photoplay's* feature "Some Palaces the Fans Built," made up of pictures of the most extravagant homes of many of the most successful actors in film, is obviously geared toward engaging the spectator vicariously in a spectacle of consumption.[26]

Rivaling the home as a mark of wealth and consumption was the motorcar. At a time when automobiles were still extremely scarce and gasoline prohibitively expensive, the stars must have seemed like extravagant pioneering spirits, appearing as they did in article after article in the latest and most exotic models. An article in *Motion Picture Magazine* entitled "Their Homes on Wheels," for instance, displayed pictures of Edna Payne in her "Hupmobile," May Allison in her Cabriolette, Harold Lockwood in his "King Eight," and May Allison in her unidentified "snow-white car."[27] These were all fabulous cars, evidence in and of themselves of wealth, success, and consumer happiness. Yet they did not exist merely as possessions; they were also, equally importantly, instruments of a particularly modern recreational activity. The private lives of the stars were made up not only of familial alliances and possessions, but also of a series of activities outside of the studio. There were thus constant references to the stars' hobbies. Some of these consisted of "refining influences," such as reading literature, playing musical instruments, attending the theater, and some common activities, such as cooking, embroidery, and receiving friends. Yet by far the most popular hobby, the one most consistently mentioned, was motoring. Questions about motoring were asked almost reflexively in celebrity interviews and were invariably answered in the affirmative. Even Blanche Sweet, who insisted that she hated cooking and had no hobbies at all, had to admit that she enjoyed motoring and that it was "really very thrilling to drive downtown in the traffic."[28] A few months after this statement was published a full-page photograph of Sweet and her car appeared in *Photoplay* with the caption "They Burn Up Roads around Los Angeles." "When Blanche Sweet isn't pouting, crying or otherwise emoting in the Lasky studios she's probably out whirling her big Italian car through the incense of orange blossoms on the beautiful California highways."[29] The pleasures of leisure are, with motoring, quite explicitly the pleasures of sensual pursuit. The erotic overtones in the following excerpt from an interview with Herbert Prior and Mabelle Trunnelle are clear: " 'There isn't anything I would prefer to running an automobile if you [Mabelle Trunnelle] were in it,' he declared. Then they both laughed. Anyone who has seen them speeding along the Florida roads, with Prior at the wheel and Mrs. Prior, cheeks flaming, eyes shining, lips parted in sheer ecstasy of enjoyment, knows that the Priors' mania is motoring."[30]

The ecstasy of the stars was unashamedly celebrated in the fan magazines as long as it was a very specific kind of ecstasy. As we have seen, the presentation of the star's behavior was, in some ways, limited by traditional codes of morality. Yet, in another respect, the star was worshipped as a creature completely free to express him or herself by pursuing the pleasures afforded by the emergent consumer culture. The star emerged, to use Leo Lowenthal's famous phrase, as an idol of consumption.[31]

At least two other aspects of the star's identity vis à vis consumerism should be noted. First, a number of articles appeared throughout the teens and early twenties that demonstrated the star's taste and extravagance in fashion. Players such as Florence Hackett and Norma Talmadge were presented as models for the way the women of the country should dress. Second, stars began to appear in advertising in the teens, even more explicitly promoting the joys of consumption. Female stars appeared, for instance, endorsing beauty products.[32]

A final aspect of the star's identity, though one not developed very elaborately, was explicitly political. There were frequent comments by the stars on the suffrage movement both pro and con, and occasional disparate remarks about topics such as the war in Europe and the competence of William Jennings Bryan.[33] The patriotic zeal of Fairbanks and Pickford after America entered the war might be included here as well.

The progressive elaboration of the player's identity changed the status of film both as signification and as a commodity. First, as I have argued, the player's identity entered into the process of the film's production of meaning; it was given as a principal source of the film's enunciation and thus as an active pole in an intersubjective relation between speaking subject and the spectator as the receiver of the message. Some remarks about the specific features of the star film's textuality follow from the discussion in this chapter. It is possible, at this point, to focus on the way the star's identity was deployed in the fiction film and describe the particular mode of reception it involved.

When speaking of the positioning of the "I" in an enunciative situation it is useful to make a distinction between the aesthetic text and everyday discourse. Within a normal conversation the "I" tends away from ambiguity and toward a more habitually accepted and stable reference. This is often not the case in aesthetic discourse, which may produce its effect by problematizing the normal enunciative situation. A simple example of this is found in many first-person novels in which the "I" can be assigned alternatively to a character, a fictional narrator, an implied author, or a real author. Within the arena of subjectivity established by the star system there is an even more extraordinary play of shifting levels of identity. At one level, the person appearing in the film is a fictional character with a set of traits and a narrative function; at another, that person is an actor associated with certain techniques and an aesthetic heritage; the person may also be someone who has appeared in a number of films and may have—by virtue of this—an "image" or a "personality." At yet another level that person may have a private life that has been publicized and thus an identity completely removed from his or her appearance in films. It may be noted that these different levels of identity correspond roughly to the different stages of the early star system that have been discussed here: actor, picture personality, and star.

These various identities are attached to the same body in the film, but they are not contained there because they are to varying degrees irreconcilable. The process and the pleasure of the star film involves the negotiation of these collapsing levels of identity. An example will clarify this point. The play of different levels of identity is especially clear in Mary Pickford's 1915 film *Stella Maris*. Pickford plays two characters in the film, a beautiful rich girl and a homely young orphan. In one scene the orphan sits sadly in front of a mirror contemplating her image and comparing it unfavorably to that of the rich girl, Stella. The play of identity is extremely complex here, but two or three of its more obvious aspects can be noted. The orphan girl's contemplation of her identity in many ways doubles a similar contemplation of her identity on the spectator's part. For one thing, she is played by the same person as the character she would like to be like; a single identity thus subtends an expression of utter difference at the level of the fiction. Her orphanhood, misery, and poorness are not only opposed to the traits of the character Stella, but also just as diametrically to the traits of Pickford insofar as the spectator is aware of her private life. Here, a woman who lives in the utmost luxury presents herself as a pitiful and poor little girl. The fact that she does this certainly calls attention to her acting, but this, her ability to manipulate certain techniques, itself exists apart from her private identity. The mirror in the scene does not reflect the orphan's identity, it refracts it.

This example illustrates one of the central points that I have put forward in this book. The star system has functioned since its inception to lead us beyond the *enoncé* and outside of the self-enclosed text to a contemplation of the enunciation and particularly to a contemplation of the identity of an enunciating subject. This identity is never a simple one. It exists as something of an enigma, something always in the process of being figured out (and never finally figured out). In fact, I have argued that a kind of hermeneutic characterizes the mode of reception set in place with the star system. In reading the film the spectator is confronted with a series of questions directed toward the discovery of the reality behind the representation. With the star system, this "reality" (which could be understood in other, more analytically sophisticated ways) is reduced largely to a question of the "true" identity of the actor as the film's source. This source is not, as we have seen, merely a formal figure, but rather the subject of an extremely extensive textual elaboration. I have presented the early history of this elaboration in some detail, but I have also attempted to show the way this elaboration transformed the textuality of the American film. The various levels at which one could seize the identity of those appearing in films—as character, as actor, as picture personality, and as star—were gradually constructed over the course of the period I have covered.

This symbolic identity became a dominant site of attention, both within films and in the discourse that surrounded them. It would be a mistake to ignore the extent to which the symbolic is intertwined with the economic in this phenomenon. The actor's identity, by virtue of its symbolic status, functioned as an economic category in a system of exchange. Thus another, final point must be stressed here. The emergence of the star system changed the status of film as a commodity.

The previous discussion of the early promotions of picture personalities should give a clear indication of how suddenly and how systematically the players' identities became a chief means of product differentiation. The question of what people paid for when they paid to see films is a complex one; people undoubtedly went to the movies for a number of reasons. However, it is clear that with the star system they began to pay particularly for an experience of the actor's identity. This became a dominant aesthetic focus during these years. At the same time, of course, and inextricably, it became the dominant means of film promotion.

As we have seen, the actor's identity was essentially an intertextual one based on connections between films and between other kinds of discourse. These connections had an economic as well as textual function. The star system worked to construct a particular kind of consumer around the star as commodity, what is perhaps most commonly referred to as the fan. Since the player's identity could not be fully garnered from the individual film, the spectator had to enter into a regular habit of moviegoing to fully experience that identity. The spectator's activity—decoding meaning—became contingent on a pattern of repetitive consumer behavior that followed the actor's appearance from film to film. The advertisement of a particular player in a film set up two distinct sets of expectations that the consumer could bank on in returning to the cinema. First, the film would enter into a relationship of continuity with previous experiences of the actor's identity; something familiar would be repeated. The star system provided not only a means of differentiating films but also a means of grouping them, experiencing their interconnections and even their history. Second, the advertisement would always carry with it at least implicitly the promise that the film would extend and elaborate—not merely repeat—the actor's identity and that a previously concealed truth about the actor might be revealed. The hermeneutic that characterized the star system had obvious ramifications for the star's status as commodity. One could pursue answers for the many questions produced about the star's identities, but this would involve paying to see films on a regular basis.

Since the identity of the actor was elaborated not only in films but also in fan magazines and the general press, it remained in process long after the individual film's production of meaning had ended. Star discourse thus worked to extend the contact between the spectator/consumer and the cinema at large. More accurately, it might be said that this discourse extended the boundaries of the cinema as institution so that it could more fully occupy people's lives. For instance, subscribers to many newspapers in 1915 were presented with a daily syndicated article by Mary Pickford. These columns certainly advertised her current films, but more generally, they advertised all Pickford films, all star films, and perhaps all other films as well. That is, they promoted an experience of the cinema that was based on the performer's identity. It is important to note that they did so by providing a part of that experience. People reading a newspaper or magazine story about a star were experiencing the cinema—or at least one of its principal aspects. They were able, obliged perhaps, to continue their search for the truth of the actor's identity after the movie, between films.

Thus, star discourse involved people in the cinema outside of the movie theaters. This involvement was not sufficient unto itself, however, and thus star discourse worked to reinforce their status as film consumers. All star discourse was incomplete or at least contingent; it referred one to a more primary object, the moving pictures in which the players' identities would be more vividly and more dramatically staged. Thus, star discourse worked to lead the reader back to the theater and into the economic exchange that was central to the functioning of the cinema as business and as institution. In short, it worked to produce an exchange value that would match the price of a movie ticket.

NOTES

1. *Motion Picture*, Aug. 1916, p. 59.
2. *Photoplay*, Oct. 1916, p. 106.
3. Ibid., Jan. 1914, p. 55. The story began in the Nov. 1913 issue.
4. Ibid., Mar. 1914, p. 105.
5. Carolyn Penelope See, *The Hollywood Novel: An Historical and Critical Study* (Ph.D. diss., University of California, Los Angeles, 1963).
6. See Mendel Kohansky, *The Disreputable Profession: The Actor in Society* (Westport, Conn.: Greenwood Press, 1984), and Benjamin McArthur, *Actors and American Culture, 1880–1920* (Philadelphia: Temple University Press, 1984).
7. *Photoplay*, Sept. 1914, p. 70.
8. See Kohansky and McArthur for references to a number of the

theatrical scandals of the nineteenth century; for a more detailed discussion of this see Garth Jowett, *Film: The Democratic Art* (Boston: Little, Brown, 1976).

9. *Motion Picture*, Feb. 1915, pp. 85–88.

10. *Photoplay*, Dec. 1915, p. 130.

11. Ibid., Apr. 1916, p. 38; Sept. 1914, p. 59.

12. Ibid., Jan. 1915, p. 114.

13. Ibid., May 1917, p. 67.

14. Nick Browne, "Griffith's Family Discourse: Griffith and Freud," *Quarterly Review of Film Studies* 6, no. 1 (Winter 1981), pp. 67–80. Reprinted in *Home Is Where the Heart Is: Studies in Melodrama and the Woman's Film*, ed. Christine Gledhill (London: British Film Institute, 1987), pp. 223–35.

15. *Moving Picture World*, Dec. 2, 1911, p. 734; *Photoplay*, Dec. 1912, p. 100.

16. *Photoplay*, Mar. 1912, p. 72.

17. Ibid., June 1915, p. 154; Aug. 1915, p. 154; Sept. 1916, p. 143.

18. Ibid., June 1917, pp. 75–76.

19. *Motion Picture*, Mar. 1916, p. 111.

20. *Photoplay*, Apr. 1914, p. 83; June 1914, p. 58; July 1915, p. 134; *Moving Picture News*, Feb. 14, 1914, p. 52; *Motion Picture*, June 1916, p. 53; July 1919, pp. 40–41.

21. *Photoplay*, Mar. 1919, p. 31.

22. For a particularly good example of this see "Mothers of the Movies: Some of Them Are Real Mothers," *Photoplay*, June 1915, pp. 38–39. Also see "Alice Joyce and Her Baby," *Photoplay*, June 1916, p. 38; *Photoplay*, Dec. 1916, pp. 56–57; for instance, we are told that "you never hear Anna Little complain about the way the eggs are scrambled. Her mother supervises all the cooking in the Santa Barbara bungalow of the Little family and she believes that a person cannot act properly unless properly fed." See *Photoplay*, Dec. 1916, pp. 56–57.

23. *Photoplay*, Jan. 1914, pp. 72–73.

24. Ibid., June 1916, p. 51; Jan. 1916, p. 152; Oct. 1918, p. 56.

25. Lary May, *Screening Out the Past: The Birth of Mass Culture and the Motion Picture Industry* (New York: Oxford University Press, 1980).

26. *Photoplay*, Oct. 1918, p. 56; Aug. 1917, pp. 75–76.

27. *Motion Picture*, Apr. 1916, pp. 89–94.

28. *Photoplay*, Apr. 1915, pp. 88–90.

29. Ibid., Nov. 1915, p. 33.

30. Ibid., June 1914, pp. 60–61.

31. Leo Lowenthal, "The Triumph of Mass Idols," in *Literature, Popular Culture, and Society,* ed. Leo Lowenthal (Englewood Cliffs, N.J.: Prentice-Hall, 1961), pp. 109–40.

32. See, for instance, "Clothes: A Chat with Florence Hackett," *Motion Picture Story,* Jan. 1914, p. 101; "Spring Hats Worn by the Movie Stars," *Photoplay,* Apr. 1915, p. 96; and "Look Who's Been Shopping," *Photoplay,* Jan. 1920, p. 33; see *Photoplay,* June 1914, p. 168; Apr. 1918, pp. 103, 105.

33. See *Motion Picture Story,* Apr. 1914, p. 111; Aug. 1913, p. 121; July 1913, p. 114; and *Photoplay,* June 1914, p. 58.

Star Scandals

One thing I do love about pictures, and that is the fact that so far we haven't heard a word about the "temptations of the movies." Not a solitary comment has been made against their perfect propriety. That is really exceedingly nice. The temptations that are supposed to beset unfortunate maidenhood on the stage have been so thoroughly thrashed through that apparently nothing of the sort is left for the "movies." If we shall only escape the overdone topic then I think we shall owe a large debt of gratitude to the pictures. But some sensationalist is bound to appear in the not too distant future and tell feverish histories of the terrible "atmosphere" that the "movie" artist inhales.[1]

THE star scandals of the twenties represent the next systematic extension of the player's identity. As we have seen, writing of the teens projected a very conventional view of the stars' family lives. The divorces and murders that occupied much of the writing on the stars in the twenties obviously contradicted this view. With the star scandals the star became a site for the representation of moral transgression and social unconventionality.

Writing on this aspect of the star system's development usually focuses on three particular scandals: Roscoe "Fatty" Arbuckle's alleged murder of Virginia Rappe in 1921, William Desmond Taylor's mysterious murder in 1922, and Wallace Reid's death by drug overdose in 1923.[2] These were indeed the most sensational and most significant scandals of the period, but they were not isolated ones. In the Arbuckle, Taylor, and Reid scandals we see the eruption of three events marked not only by their sensationalism but also by their singularity. The significance of these events, however, should be understood in the context of a more general shift in the representation of stars, in the construction of their identities. This shift was underway well before Roscoe Arbuckle's party in the St. Francis Hotel.

As noted earlier, theatrical stars had traditionally been associated with scandal. The writing that first began to focus on the private lives of movie stars had noted the potential for scandal but had worked to distinguish the movie star from the theatrical star in this regard. Thus, scandal was from the beginning the repressed underside of the movie star's existence. Indeed even the earliest writing on the stars' private lives referred fairly frequently to the potential for scandal, if only to deny it as a reality. For instance, the short story "The Glory Road," examined in the last chapter, presented a villainous attack on a woman's chastity within the world of filmmaking. Although fictional scandals of this sort were always averted, there was evidence that many of the real women in Hollywood were not so lucky. In the teens there was a general expression of public concern for the fate of those women who had left their homes to become stars. Hundreds had flocked to the Los Angeles area in search of fame, and in doing so they had created a very real local problem. The economy could not support such an influx, and consequently women ended up stranded and destitute. Articles about this admitted that there were unscrupulous elements in the film community eager to take advantage of these desperate women:

> Gradually, it dawned upon the paternal city government that the pretty game of catching up with Mary had its ugly side. A faint odor of singed wings came to the official nostrils as the gleaming lamp was proudly trimmed. It needed but a careful look about to discover a number of pathetic things.

> What then is Little Miss Movie-Struck "Star" to do after three years around the studios? By this time three years of hard work have sapped her splendid vitality; she has become

accustomed to the freedom of studio life, and she suffers from the lack of restraint one observes when a company is out on location.[3]

These are fairly strong generalizations about the moral atmosphere of film production, and from them one might infer all kinds of atrocities. What is striking though is that the concern expressed for these women never departs from the most general level. One does not see stories about specific scandals—a specific woman's misfortune, or the involvement of a particular actor or producer in the exploitation of such a woman. The charges about Hollywood may have been titillating, but they were also extremely vague. In the face of the dozens of articles concretely outlining the idyllic family lives of the stars they probably carried little weight, except perhaps insofar as they kept the potential of scandal in view. They may have produced suspicions about Hollywood life, but they did not satisfy them. These charges are crucial, however, because they raised the question that underpinned much of the future development of star discourse—"Are the stars immoral?" The possibility of the star's immorality existed throughout the teens beneath the morality directly attributed to them in the press. It was this deeper truth (more hidden, more private, more sexual) that would be exposed and exploited in the twenties.

A significant shift in the representation of the star began to take place in 1920 and 1921. For the first time attention began to be focused to a significant degree on the domestic problems of the stars. It is true that some star divorces had been reported in the late teens—those of Conway Tearle, Clara Kimbell Young, Francis X. Bushman, and Douglas Fairbanks—but these divorces received scant attention and were treated like the divorces of prominent citizens from other fields. The *Chicago Tribune*, for instance, which was otherwise quite active in its treatment of the movies, gave only thirteen lines to the Fairbanks divorce. More significant, discussion of these divorces did not make its way into the entertainment pages of newspapers, into the fan magazines, or into the national magazines of the day. The conventions of star discourse were relatively unaffected by these isolated bits of "news." In the early twenties, however, those conventions changed, and references to divorce, adultery, and moral transgression became a regular feature of star discourse, a part of the formula for writing about stars. The following passages from a 1921 issue of *Photoplay* serve as evidence of the kind of writing on stars that became common during this time:

> One of Conway Tearle's former wives is suing him for more alimony. We forget which one. She says Conway is getting more money from the company for which he is making pictures than he has ever received before in his career and she wants some of it.

> Pearl White has always been persistent in her refusal to permit the public to peek into her affairs. Until she got a divorce from her husband, Wallace McCutcheon. You can keep a marriage out of the papers but you can't always soft-pedal a divorce. So when Pearl appealed to the courts to let her be Miss White again, the greatest part of her public was a bit surprised.[4]

It had long been established that the stars were different from everyone else in their beauty and wealth. The claim that they were like everyone else in their marital and sexual relations had been assiduously maintained throughout the teens, however. Around 1920 concrete evidence began to emerge in the press and fan magazines that the stars were different in this respect as well, that the potential for scandal that had hung over the industry for so long was at last being realized. An article in *Photoplay* described people talking about Mrs. Charlie Chaplin's divorce behind her back. Another article depicted the five types of movie fans, including "The Gossip" ("She knows all of the latest scandal about the stars").[5] Karl Kitchen published the results of his investigation into the morals of studio life in 1920. After denying that the exploitation of would-be actresses was in any way common, he turned his attention to divorce:

> There is a popular catch line in Southern California, "Are you married, or do you live in Los Angeles?" But this is

current because of the frequency of divorce and its attendant evils among members of the movie colony. There are doubtless quite as many divorces among cloak and suit manufacturers, if authentic statements were obtainable. Matrimonial infelicity is not peculiar to any class of people these days. And of most of the motion picture stars it may be said that if they have any faults they make virtues of them.[6]

Stories of the divorces of the stars obviously militated against the family discourse that had been so important in supporting claims that the cinema was "at its source" a healthy phenomenon. What was lost in moral integrity was, no doubt, gained in glamour; indeed, most stars were able to turn the revelation of their personal problems to their advantage.

It should be stressed that the divorces of 1920 and 1921 were tame and trivial compared to the scandals that followed. They are significant not for the effect they had on individual actors' careers, nor for the repercussions they had in the industry at large, but instead as evidence of yet another expansion of the kind of knowledge that constituted the identity of the star. Exposés on the real lives of the stars would no longer be limited to stories of success, security, and marital bliss; transgression, betrayal, restlessness, and loss entered into the dramatic formula.

The Pickford-Moore divorce, which was the most important and widely reported divorce of 1920–21, deserves special mention. The *New York Times* reported in March 1920:

> Mary Pickford, to whom was granted a divorce from Owen Moore at Minden, Nevada, on the grounds of desertion, has been separated from Mr. Moore for several years. They had worked at the same studios, but never in the same company, since their separation. Miss Pickford and her family have always declined to discuss her marital affairs, but because of her religious faith it was a surprise in motion picture circles when word of the decree was received.[7]

Later, charges of Moore's brutality and drunkenness surfaced.

It seems particularly significant that Pickford and Moore's marital difficulties and separation had not come to light before their divorce, especially since Pickford was the most written about actor of the teens. Actually, much had been written about the couple's life together, but all of it presented a rosy picture. "Our Mary and Her Owen," for instance, appeared in late 1917, detailing in pictures and words the strong friendship that underpinned the couple's marriage.[8] The *Times* account of the divorce seems to indicate that Pickford and Moore were not even together at this time. Writing about them still fell within the bounds of other writings about star couples of the teens, presenting them as symbols of domestic bliss. By the time of their divorce, however, those bounds were beginning to give way.

Immediately after the divorce Pickford announced that she would never marry again, that she would "devote the remainder of her life to moving pictures." However, by the end of the month she had married Douglas Fairbanks in a Los Angeles ceremony. The quick marriage raised suspicions that the couple had been involved in an affair for some time. In fact, according to some sources those suspicions had existed for years, though they had not, to my knowledge, been directly voiced in the press. After the Pickford-Fairbanks marriage, an article in *Photoplay* claimed that rumors of the romance had begun after a report that Fairbanks had saved Pickford from injury in a studio accident. While he carried her to safety, the report supposedly read, Pickford put her arms around his neck. "The eager tongue of gossip began to wag. The friendship of Mary Pickford and Douglas Fairbanks was given a sinister significance."[9] An article announcing the marriage knowingly offered the following overview of the situation: "The denouement of the Mary Pickford-Douglas Fairbanks matrimonial tangles will cause little surprise to the countless followers of these two movie stars, whose mutual romance has been the subject of gossip for years."[10] Such statements give some credence to the notion that scandal was the repressed underside of star discourse of the teens, that fans may have been prompted to imagine situations that the family discourse of writing on stars attempted to disavow. Fairbanks and Pickford had appeared together in countless publicity photos (specifically for the war bond drives and the formation of United Artists). Moreover, they were the most idealized man and woman in moving pictures, who, because of that, could easily be imagined as an ideal couple. Finally, those who followed the newspapers closely (it was not reported in *Photoplay* or *Moving Picture World*) might have known that Fairbanks had been charged by his wife with adultery and divorced in 1918 and that the corespondent's name had never been made public. These factors taken together provided certain grounds for suspicion for fans willing to use their imaginations and make the necessary inferences. Yet those suspicions would proceed until the wedding without the direct confirmation of the press and fan magazines, which seemed to ignore anything that might have been going on between the two actors. In any case, whether Pickford and Fairbanks's extramarital involvement had been widely rumored or not, the couple's marriage so soon after Pickford's divorce made the story of the previous years pretty obvious to anyone who gave it much thought.[11]

What is remarkable about all of this is how seamlessly the "sinister" aspects of the Pickford-Fairbanks affair were recuperated in a family discourse and how completely the couple escaped the stigma of scandal. Indeed, all of the complications of this affair had little effect on either Pickford's or Fairbanks's image. In fact, the opposite could be said to be true. Within months Pickford and Fairbanks were being touted as the country's ideal couple, whose conventional lifestyle could stand as an example for millions. "'Our life is simple and frank,'" said Mary, three months after the divorce, "'just an old fashioned sort of life.'" Pickford and Fairbanks became commentators on the "art" of marriage. And, incredibly enough, the couple became yet another symbol of the healthiness of moving picture life as opposed to the danger of stage life:

Here in New York Fannie Hurst, having consulted her engagement book and found the evening free mutters madly, "What is the name of that man I married? I ought to have his telephone number somewhere." Out in Hollywood California, a little woman with golden hair puts the chops on the stove and wonders with a sigh if her adorable fellow will be late. The telephone rings and he tells her he will be on hand for dinner in twenty minutes accompanied by fourteen guests. . . . Married life under such conditions is more than art. It's work.[12]

"The Wooing of Mary Pickford," which appeared in June 1920, recounted the couple's romance, presenting it not as a scandal but as "one of the great love stories of all time." Pickford and Fairbanks were portrayed as suffering souls who had never found true happiness in life until they found sympathy, companionship, and, finally, love in each other. Pickford appeared as a typically melodramatic heroine in the story; in fact, the article claimed that anyone who knew her pictures could see that her real-life "poignant sadness" was reflected there.[13] This sadness had disappeared with her marriage to Fairbanks. The article attacked those who looked toward the more sensational aspects of the story and charged that they were nonbelievers in romance.

Fairbanks's and Pickford's behavior prior to their marriage definitely exceeded the limits of the conventions of the day. However, the pair completely escaped the stigma of scandal, probably because of the public's extreme sympathy for these actors, the presentation of their behavior in terms of personal fulfillment, and the absence of any explicit references to sexual infidelity. The affair existed completely apart from the scandals that would sweep the industry in the next couple of years, so much so that an article in *Photoplay* in 1922, responding to the scandals and begging new stars to behave themselves, could single out Pickford as the best example to follow.[14]

On September 12, 1921, a United News Service story appeared in newspapers throughout the country, announcing what would be the most shocking and most important star scandal of the twenties:

Roscoe [Fatty] Arbuckle, next to Charlie Chaplin the children's favorite film comedian, but privately known to the gay motion picture colonies of Los Angeles as a thorough Bohemian, occupies a cell in the city jail, held without bail in connection with the death of Miss Virginia Rappe, a beautiful film actress, which followed the latest and probably the last of the famous private Arbuckle jollifications. The party was held last Monday, Miss Rappe was removed from Arbuckle's suite in the luxurious St. Francis hotel that afternoon suffering agony. She died after lingering for days for treatment for alcoholism, an erroneous diagnosis. Her death is now claimed to have been due to an internal rupture which caused peritonitis.[15]

By 1921 Arbuckle was one of Paramount's most important stars. His humor depended to a large degree on his enormous bulk and excessive appetite. A 1918 article, for instance, revealed that Fatty was making a personal sacrifice for the war effort by eating only a few hams a day.[16] This image of excess lent credence to the implications of sexual debauchery that arose as a result of the investigation into Rappe's death. The image of an uncontrollable Arbuckle crushing the young actress with his weight could not have been far from most people's minds.

The "gin jollification" (a term apparently coined by Arbuckle and taken up widely in the press) was attended by Rappe; her friend Mrs. B. M. Delmont; her manager Al Semnacher; Ira Fortlouis, a New York wardrobe salesman; Alice Blake, a San Francisco café entertainer; Lowell Sherman, a friend of Arbuckle with a financial interest in moving pictures; Fred Fishbeck, a director; Zey Pyvron, a local showgirl; and others who came and went throughout the course of the festivities. During the party, in Arbuckle's room away from the rest of the guests, Rappe began screaming in pain. According to most of the witnesses' accounts, though not all, Arbuckle was alone with her at the time. Eleven bruises were found on her body. Doctors later testified that "external force had caused a rupture of the bladder, resulting in peritonitis, which caused the death of Miss Rappe."[17] The district attorney immediately charged Arbuckle with murder, though he was eventually indicted only for manslaughter. After three trials a jury acquitted Arbuckle.

The scandal that erupted had less to do with Arbuckle's guilt or innocence than with the picture of Hollywood life that emerged

during the investigation and trial. Arbuckle and Rappe were immediately pictured as something other than moral homebodies:

> Miss Rappe became prominent in Chicago in 1913, when
> she announced that she was earning $4000 a year as a model
> and urged other girls to try that profession. A year later she
> was again in the limelight due to reports that she and an-
> other beautiful young woman had presented a dance called
> the "nightly tango" in a steamship en voyage to France. She
> startled Paris with fur anklets, one pink, pantalettes and a
> bouquet of fruit instead of flowers.

> All down the glittering gold coast of the Los Angeles motion
> picture colony, peopled by men and women of humble begin-
> ning suddenly possessed of fabulous wealth because of a
> pretty face, a fat physique, wavy hair or a simpering smile,
> Fatty Arbuckle is known for the "parties" he gives. In the
> Hollywood colony near Los Angeles, the announcement that
> Fatty Arbuckle would "throw a dinner" was the signal for
> rejoicing by those who appreciated that sort of merriment. It
> meant oblivious relief from the grind of the movie lot. And
> no guest, however blase, could go through an Arbuckle affair
> without finding a new thrill. His famous dog wedding is
> historic in Hollywood, where a party must be a party to be
> noticed at all.[18]

The details of the party that emerged during the investigation
and trial were still more shocking. "Liquor was served. . . . There
was a phonograph in the room discoursing current jazz. Arbuckle, in
a dressing gown over his silk pajamas and with bare feet shoved into
slippers, sat near Miss Rappe, 'kidding her,' during the afternoon.
One statement says they sat together on a settee."[19] Mrs. B. B.
Delmont, who made the initial allegations against Arbuckle, admitted having ten drinks during the party. At one point, "warm with
dance," she had changed into a pair of the men's pajamas. (Later, just
after the first trial, she was charged and convicted of bigamy.) One
witness claimed that when Rappe began screaming Arbuckle had

Norma Talmadge's House. (The Museum of Modern Art, Film Stills Archive)

Mary Pickford in *Stella Maris*. (The Museum of Modern Art, Film Stills Archive)

Mary Pickford and Douglas Fairbanks. (The Museum of Modern Art, Film Stills Archive)

Wallace Reid with son and collie.
(The Museum of Modern Art,
Film Stills Archive)

Wallace Reid's funeral. (The Museum of Modern Art, Film Stills Archive)

Fatty Arbuckle. (The Museum of Modern Art, Film Stills Archive)

Theda Bara. (Billy Rose Theatre Collection, The New York Public Library at Lincoln Center, Astor, Lenox, and Tilden Foundations)

Theda Bara in a publicity still for *Cleopatra*. (Billy Rose Theatre Collection, The New York Public Library at Lincoln Center, Astor, Lenox, and Tilden Foundations)

rushed out of the room wearing Rappe's panama hat and pajamas soaked through with sweat. When the assistant manager of the hotel got to Arbuckle's suite he found him carrying Rappe, who was nude to the waist, from his room to another. Rappe's clothing was introduced in court and carefully described by the press: "a green silk dress, rumpled and soiled; dainty print silk underwear torn almost to shreds, a pair of silk garters, a hat and a cloak." A nurse claimed that Rappe had told her positively that there had been "intimacy" with Arbuckle. Al Semnacher charged that Arbuckle admitted to him that he had tortured Rappe.[20]

One of the oddest aspects of the Arbuckle affair is the position *Photoplay* took regarding it. *Photoplay* was the most active magazine in promulgating information about the lives, loves, and possessions of the stars. And yet when what was arguably the biggest star story ever broke they ignored it. Neither the crime nor the trial were reported in 1921. Arbuckle, however, was not ignored. In September, the month the incident occurred, an interview of Arbuckle appeared, entitled "Love Confessions of a Fat Man." The interviewer, Adela Rogers St. John, described the bedroom in which the interview took place as well as Arbuckle's pongee pajamas ("I shall never be able to estimate just what percentage of effect they had on me—those pongee pajamas") before revealing that Arbuckle's bedroom was a studio set and the "seventeen stage carpenters, thirteen electricians and a few stray cameramen" acted as chaperones.[21] St. John portrays Arbuckle as a kind of sex symbol and then allows him the chance to voice his opinions on being fat ("'The fat man as lover is going to be the best seller on the market for the next few years'"), women ("'A man's ideal is most of the things most men want to come home to—slippers, drawn curtains, a bright fire, peace, praise, comfort, and a good, hot dinner'"), and marital fidelity ("'Fat men are inclined to be faithful. It's often a form of laziness, you know'"). There is even a line about murder: "'Fat men make the best husbands because . . . it is very hard to either murder or be murdered by a fat man.'"[22] The interview was supposed to be humorous, but given Rappe's death, it could have only been read as grotesquely ironic. I think that one can probably assume that the September issue was published before Arbuckle's party. This, however, does not explain the inclusion of an article by Arbuckle in the October issue of the magazine. In "What the Well-Dressed Man Will Wear" Arbuckle reviewed the latest fashions from Paris in a fairly straightforward and serious manner. An accompanying picture presented him as quite a dandy. The article must have supported people's inclination to view his taste for clothes as just another indication of a life of excess. Some may have recalled that a wardrobe salesman had been one of the guests at his "gin jollification." The October issue also included a report on the censors' trip to Hollywood the previous summer and noted that Arbuckle had headed the big table at Madame Nazimova's party for the group.

In short, *Photoplay* ignored the scandal reported in every newspaper in the country and continued to publish very traditional, uncontroversial stories about Arbuckle. One could argue that "What the Well-Dressed Man Will Wear" was ready for publication prior to the scandal and that the magazine decided that by publishing it they could capitalize on the sudden curiosity about the actor. Yet a story about what "really" happened in the St. Francis Hotel would have certainly drawn more attention. To my mind, this exclusion demonstrates the magazine's interest in maintaining the boundaries of star discourse discussed in the last chapter. It had, until this time, been able to exert a strong control over information produced about stars, filling its pages with tales of morality, family life, and the privileges of new wealth. Publicity departments and publicity agents had gladly cooperated in this venture, feeding *Photoplay* and the other fan magazines just this sort of information. The details of the Arbuckle scandal fell radically outside of the bounds of what had previously been permissible in star discourse. The regulation of knowledge that had been effected fairly unproblematically since the middle teens was disrupted and to a degree began to break down.

It is tempting to argue that the star scandals represent a radical break with the terms of previous star discourse. The scandals did appear, after all, as a kind of repudiation of the picture of the stars' family lives that had been put forward in the teens—the star would no longer function as a guarantor of the cinema's morality. Throughout the teens the star had served both as publicity and public relations, but in the twenties, its value as public relations was greatly tarnished. The star became a site of struggle between reformers and the industry, the subject of social controversy. The cinema lost a degree of control over star discourse as newspaper writers, reformers, and politicians entered into a debate over the nature of the film star's identity. A number of voices began to speak the star, many of them from a position of strong antipathy toward the cinema.

Many of the early actions of Will Hays, head of the newly formed Motion Picture Producers and Distributors of America (MMPDA), demonstrate the extent to which the scandals appeared as a crisis within the industry. The cinema had encountered the protests of reformers for most of its history, and the specter of censorship had hung over the industry since at least 1909 when the mayor of New York City temporarily closed all movie theaters and the National Board of Censorship was formed. The reform movement gained strength throughout the teens, and by 1920 the passage of the Eighteenth Amendment proved (though it was to most already quite clear) that the movement had the power to prompt sweeping social changes. The moving picture industry had been fighting scattered attempts at state censorship since at least the middle teens. By the time of the Arbuckle scandal the problem had become extreme: censorship bills were under discussion in thirty-six states.[23]

The Arbuckle scandal intensified the industry's problems. The image of moral healthiness presented so insistently in star discourse during the teens had in fact functioned as an argument against censorship. The movies occasionally transgressed traditional norms (they did so increasingly in the late teens), but the public was constantly assured that the movies were, "at their source" a healthy phenomenon and that the people who made them led exemplary lives. Star discourse clearly contradicted characterizations of the cinema as an instrument of evil and thus acted as a palliative to reform efforts.

The Arbuckle scandal dealt a serious blow to this illusion of moral rectitude. Reformers used it to make broad attacks on the stars and the industry in general. Arbuckle, after all, had to all appearances been morally upright himself, only to be exposed as a libertine. It was easy to assume that the public had been more generally duped by fan magazines and press agents and that, behind the surface respectability of Hollywood, there were countless similarly ugly stories. (A play of surface and depth had of course characterized the star system; here it is turned, momentarily at least, against the publicity apparatus itself.)

The revelations about Arbuckle and the implications about Hollywood that were readily drawn from his behavior greatly strengthened censorship efforts. First, not surprisingly, Arbuckle's films were banned in dozens of communities across the country. When it was discovered that certain exhibitors were trying to capitalize on the scandal by showing Rappe's films, they were withdrawn from distribution. More important though, the scandal fueled censorship efforts at the state level. In the case of New York, it legitimized a state censorship commission that had been quite controversial at the time of its inception.[24] By the middle of the next year the disreputable lives of the stars were being presented in arguments for censorship at the national level:

> At Hollywood is a colony of these people where debauchery, riotous living, drunkenness, ribaldry, dissipation, free love seem to be conspicuous. Many of these "stars" it is reported were formerly bartenders, butcher boys, sopers, swampers, variety actors and actresses, who may have earned $10 or $20 a week. Some of them are now paid, it is said, salaries of something like $5,000 a month or more, and they do not know what to do with their wealth, extracted from poor people in large part by 25 cent or 50 cent admission fees, except to spend it in riotous living, dissipation, and high rolling. These are some of the characters from whom the young people of today are deriving a large part of their education, views of life, and character forming habits. From these sources our young people gain much of their views of life, inspiration and education. Rather a poor source, is it not? It looks as if censorship is needed, does it not?[25]

We have seen that a play of surface and depth characterized all discourse on stars. Behind the image, this discourse constantly tells us, lies something more real. The star scandals extended this play. In the teens, one could follow the intertextual paths from the films to the ulterior "reality" of those who produced them and consistently find an image that supported traditional views of moral conduct. The above passage demonstrates that with the star scandals this had changed. Behind the films lay flattering (but fictional) images of stars constructed by press agents and behind that lay a real world of moral turpitude. The regulation of knowledge that had characterized the previous years had broken down, or it was at least in crisis. The private lives of the stars had been turned against the industry itself.

The Motion Picture Producers and Distributors of America, the Hays Office, was created in part as an institutional response to this crisis. In November 1921, leaders of the industry met to decide on the appointment of a respected and well-known person to act as a figurehead for the industry.[26] Baseball had taken similar steps after the World Series scandal of 1919 by appointing the first baseball commissioner, Judge Kenesaw Mountain Landis. A Detroit reporter, in an interview with Carl Laemmle, described the role this person was to have most succinctly: "a dictator of principles, a man whose reputation shall redound to the credit of the industry."[27] On January 14, 1922, it was announced that Will Hays, a Presbyterian elder, leader of the Republican party, and, as postmaster general, a popular member of the Harding cabinet, would be accepting the position of head of the newly formed organization, The Motion Picture Producers and Distributors of America.

It should be noted that the censorship threats and the star scandals were not the only—and probably not even the principal—impetus for the creation of the Hays Office. Much of the writing that accompanied Hays's appointment in fact viewed the industry's desire for a unified system of distribution as the principal factor. But, even though Hays was hired to accomplish a number of tasks, his most visible function related to the star scandals and the threat of censorship. For most, his success or failure would be judged by the degree to which he could counter censorship efforts and give the cinema a new moral respectability. And in this regard, Hays seems to have succeeded. Three state censorship bills were rejected in 1922, eighteen in 1923, two in 1924, and fourteen in 1925.[28]

Shortly after assuming his new role as head of the MPPDA, Hays made his most famous decision regarding the morality of the stars by banning the distribution of Arbuckle's films.[29] A document in the Hays Collection at the Indiana State Library demonstrates the cooperative nature of this decision. On Lasky stationery, it is signed by Hays and initialed by the other parties listed:

> After consultation at length with Mr. Nicholas Schenck, representing Mr. Joseph Schenck, the producers, and Mr. Adolph Zukor and Mr. Jesse Lasky, of Famous Players Corporation, the distributors, I will state that at my request they have canceled all showings and all bookings of the Arbuckle films. They do this that the whole matter may have the consideration that its importance warrants, and the action is taken notwithstanding the fact that they have nearly ten thousand contracts in force for the Arbuckle pictures.[30]

This self-sacrificing gesture on the producers and distributors' part served as a demonstration of good faith that they truly intended to cooperate in reforming the movies. It also seemed to demonstrate that Hays was not, as many claimed, merely a figurehead for an industry intent on continuing with business as usual; he had taken decisive action and gotten results. Of course, this was neither a grand sacrifice nor a decisive action. Arbuckle films, where they were still allowed, clearly functioned against the best interests of the industry at large and the specific concerns involved. But the ban was nevertheless a strong first step in a series of public relations efforts regarding the star.

The fact that these efforts continued is evident in the following telegram Hays sent to William Fox three days after the Arbuckle decision:

> Will you please send the following telegram to your studios and production department. QUOTE We are solidly back of

the official New York City Popularity Contest raising funds for poor of New York City STOP Urge every individual with company to bend every energy for success of drive means much to our entire industry in Los Angeles as well as New York STOP Do anything and everything to arouse enthusiasm UNQUOTE Please sign this telegram with your name.[31]

At a board meeting on April 7, 1922, the MPPDA considered William H. Crawford's offer to write a magazine article defending the morals of the "movie folks."[32] To my knowledge, the article by Crawford never appeared but other, similar ones did. There is no direct evidence that Hays had anything to do with these articles, but it is, I believe, a revealing coincidence that two of the most prominent ones were written by Hays's friends George Ade (who had been chairman of the Indiana State Council of Defense's publicity committee when Hays had headed the organization during World War I) and Otis Skinner (with whom Hays, according to his memoirs, had "pleasant relations"). Ade's "Answering Wild-Eyed Questions about the Movie Stars in Hollywood" appeared in *American Magazine* in May 1922. The article admitted that some of the stars had been spoiled by their sudden success but presented the following picture of life in Hollywood: "The general average of morality between Santa Barbara and San Diego is about what you might expect to find at a Wednesday-evening prayer meeting in Bethlehem, Pennsylvania."[33] He claimed that the stories of sin in Hollywood were usually fictions created by actors and their press agents who "made the mistake of assuming that almost any kind of publicity is desirable."[34] In effect, he upped the ante in the play of surface and depth described earlier; behind the apparent sinfulness of Hollywood lay a world that was quite conventional after all.

One of the industry's actions vis à vis the stars' morals is important to note here, though it was not instigated by Hays. During 1922 the inclusion of morality clauses in stars' contracts probably became standard practice. These clauses permitted the dismissal of any actor whose conduct hurt the company or the actor's own marketability.

The Arbuckle scandal had demonstrated that one could be a top attraction one day and completely unmarketable the next. The morality clause protected the studio in the event of a career-ending scandal. It also perhaps encouraged the stars to be more careful in the conduct of their private lives, since they could legally be discharged if they made a single mistake.

James Quirk (editor of *Photoplay*), in his April 1922 open letter to Will Hays, suggested that "in every motion picture contract there should be a clause similar to the one in the new Goldwyn contract, providing for the immediate discharge of any actor whose private life reflects discredit on the company." The same month *Literary Digest* reported that the magazine *Camera* had suggested character bonds for actors. And by May, morality clauses were being "written into contracts." When the Actor's Equity Association worked with Hays and the producers toward a standard actor's contract in early 1923 a morality clause was part of the package.[35]

When Hays made his first trip to Hollywood in July 1922 many imagined that he would clean house and rid the industry of its bad elements. In his memoirs Hays noted that because of this the Hollywood community saw him as their adversary, not their ally. The point of his trip, he claimed, was to correct this impression and convince the industry to work toward common goals. Thus, he made no significant efforts at reform. In fact, his statements that related to the star scandals followed the course that Ade's and Skinners's articles had by defending Hollywood against its detractors. A *New York Times* article, for instance, quoted Hays as saying that he had "failed to find the horrors of Hollywood," implying, of course, that they did not exist.[36] A later statement admitted more but still struck a defensive posture. It also flattered the journalistic profession that controlled the amount of attention the sins of the stars received:

> Hays summed up his findings on the night life and the goings on that people were so eager to hear all about by saying, "the movies are in their infancy. Nothing is wrong with the moving pictures—except youth. Whatever mistakes have been made—and no one denies that there may have been

mistakes—were the errors of youth. Picture play making is a matter of less than 20 years of age—and it really cannot be expected fairly to have the splendid stability, poise and standards of, for example, the press, which has reached its present state only after 600 years.[37]

Hays made a second trip to Hollywood in December. In his memoirs he characterizes this trip mainly as an effort to organize the West Coast office of the MPPDA. Yet newspapers presented it as a moral crusade; the names of prominent stars had recently surfaced in a New York drug investigation, and it was claimed that Hays wanted to deal with the problem of drug addiction in Hollywood before it led to a public scandal.[38]

It is often difficult to determine whether Hays took the actions he was reported to take, whether these reported actions were merely publicity for the MPPDA, or whether they were fantasies of those who wished to empower Hays to further the cause of reform. In August, for instance, a report had circulated that Hays had interceded in a domestic quarrel between W. S. Hart and his wife, but he had failed to prevent their separation; both Hart and Hays denied the report.[39] Although this level of interference seems absurd, one cannot be absolutely certain that it did not take place. A greater degree of uncertainty attends the reports of Hays's drug investigation. It is indeed difficult to determine if Hays actually conducted such an investigation on his second trip to Hollywood. However, it is perhaps just as important that the public was led to believe that this was what he was doing and that action was being taken to clean up Hollywood:

Hays told the United Press that his mission in Hollywood is not to hold a post-mortem or act as a detective, but to work constructively from within to purify and better the film game. Producers are already quietly investigating the private lives of stars. One prominent movie player who was known to be drinking and was suspected of using drugs was called before one of the biggest producers in the colony and taxed with the offense. He vehemently denied using drugs and offered to prove it. Well-known physicians were employed, and the star was stripped in the presence of producers and examined for marks of the "dope needle." No marks were found. He was then placed in the custody of a physician for three weeks it was stated. The physician never left him alone for a minute, even sleeping with him. At the end of this time the doctor reported that the star showed no signs of being an addict, inasmuch as he betrayed no craving for drugs. The actor then promised to go "on the wagon" and is reported to have been reinstated in good standing. "I am not interested in conditions in the colony during the last years, but in conditions today and tomorrow," Hays said. "My aim is to develop the amazing possibilities for good in the movies and in the types of pictures to such an extent that the bad will be automatically crowded out." He said he found very little basis for tales of scandal in the colony.[40]

Of course, Wallace Reid's death by drug overdose in January 1923 demonstrated once again that there was such a basis and detracted considerably from the credibility of Hays's public relations efforts on this front.

Both the reformers' protests and Will Hays's response to those protests reveal the extent to which the star scandals prompted a crisis within the industry, a period of threatening discontinuity with what had previously been standard practice. It is indeed tempting to argue that the star scandals represent a radical break with the terms of previous star discourse. The scandals did appear, after all, as a kind of repudiation of the picture of the stars' family lives that had been put forward in the teens. The star would no longer function as a guarantor of the cinema's morality. Throughout the teens the star had served both as publicity and public relations, but in the twenties, though its promotional value remained, its value as public relations was greatly tarnished. The star became a site of struggle between reformers and the industry, a subject of social controversy. Most significantly, the cinema lost a degree of control over star discourse as newspaper writers, reformers and politicians entered into a debate over the nature of the film star's identity. A number of voices began to speak the star, many of them from a position of strong antipathy toward the cinema.

This emphasis on the "break" in star discourse in the early twenties gains further support from a consideration of the social context of the period. There is no doubt that the broad social changes noted by Lary May—the ascendance of consumerism, the rise of sexual experimentation, and the secularization of marriage—affected and, in turn, were articulated through the star, and that the star scandals were part of (and to a degree caused by) a set of changes largely external to the cinema as an institution. There was a fascination with drugs, adultery, and scandal that extended well beyond the view of those whose attention was focused solely on the movie colony. The shift from a healthy image of the star in the teens to a more promiscuous one in the twenties can thus, in part, be viewed as the result of a broad historical shift—or to use Gilman Ostrander's term, a "revolution in morals."[41]

The metaphors of discontinuity that arise in dealing with the scandals—revolution, rupture, crisis, break—are not only unavoidable but in most respects adequate and illuminating. The period from the teens to the twenties is strongly marked by contrast, contradiction, reversal, and sudden change. This chapter has illustrated these elements of discontinuity, and I believe that the historical work that remains to be done on the star system of this period will have little use for a model of gradual change from a traditional to a more modern represented identity. However, in emphasizing the discontinuous aspects of the star scandals, we risk ignoring those ways in which the scandals entered into a relation of continuity with previous star discourse.

Two central contradictions worked against the claims of star discourse of the teens to expose the possibility of the star's immorality and keep the promise of scandal in view. They are important in establishing the preconditions (suspicion, curiosity) for the scandals of the twenties. The first involves a contradiction between the identity traced out for the actor in films (the picture personality) and the private identity constructed in star discourse (the star). Films about ideal couples and virtuous women hardly presented a challenge to the claims of star discourse. But what about films about vamps and sexually liberated women? According to Lary May the films of the teens increasingly presented a more modern view of sexuality culminating in the films of DeMille, von Stroheim, and Valentino after the war. One does not have to accept all of May's argument to recognize that these films are characterized by a less traditional morality. Of course by the time these films appeared, or shortly thereafter, star discourse had begun to concern itself with divorce and adultery as well. But what if we take the example of Theda Bara, whose 1914 film *A Fool There Was* presented her as a dangerous seductress bent on destroying men through her sexual allure? This film was a kind of Victorian morality play complete with a lesson about the dangers that lie beyond the home. But Bara's image in this film and in the films that followed it—in short her identity as a picture personality—contradicted the conventional identity traced out for stars in the popular press. This contradiction could be handled by claiming that Bara was in reality a conventional woman. Yet evidence to the contrary existed quite forcefully in her films. Her identity as a picture personality put the morality of her private life into question. Was she as she appeared on the screen or was she different? The posing of this question set the conditions for the shift in discourse in the 1920s when answers about the immorality of the stars began to be provided.[42] It may be argued that the more morally adventurous films of the teens supported suspicions that the stars were living morally adventurous lives.

A second contradiction is equally important in leading to the expansion of star discourse in the early twenties. As I have noted, there were two principal aspects of the representation of the star's private identity during the teens: an emphasis on the normalcy and morality of their domestic relations and a celebration of their pursuit of pleasure away from work. These two aspects were, in important respects, quite contradictory, one appealing to Victorian standards and the other to the self-consciously "modern." The pursuit of pleasure away from work could easily threaten traditional notions of marital commitment. Yet as long as morality was defined purely in terms of sexual conduct and pleasure purely in terms of consumption, this contradiction could be contained. Most writing on the stars during the teens attempted to keep these two regimes fairly distinct. Yet the distinction between pleasure in sex and pleasure in consumption was easily blurred. Mabelle Trunnelle's orgasmic pleasure in automobile rides provides a good example of this. Later, the connection between sex and consumption would take on a more sinister significance as, for instance, in this description of Roscoe Arbuckle's return to San Francisco where he would be charged with murder: "Arbuckle arrived back in San Francisco in his famous cream colored, custom built automobile, often compared to a pullman car, from Los Angeles where he had hastened after Miss Rappe's alarming condition caused the dispersal of the 'party.' He wore a Norfolk jacket, dark green golf breeches, woolen stockings and tan low cut shoes."[43]

The compartmentalization of material and sexual pleasures became increasingly problematic and artificial during the teens, and to some degree star discourse's obsession with the former led quite inevitably to questions about the latter. From the unbridled excess so celebrated in the stars' spending habits one could easily infer a more generalized hedonism that extended into the realm of the sexual.

Thus, the moral, 'healthy' star image of the teens was beset by contradictions that, at the very least, allowed the spectator to imagine scenarios of moral and sexual transgression. In this sense the scandals of the twenties represent not so much a reversal or a break with the teens but an actualization of something that had previously had a more virtual existence as a set of pressures, contradictions, and fantasy scenarios, something that could be located only in between the lines of conventional star discourse.

It is not merely the existence of these contradictions that connects the star discourse of the teens with the scandals of the twenties. A broader continuity can be established between the two by arguing that the scandals represent not a break with previous star discourse, but a further stage in an expansion that follows the same logic that underpinned previous expansions of the conventions of star discourse.

This logic revolves around the distinction between surface and depth and the construction of knowledge about the players as a secret. As we have seen, all discourse about those who appeared in films emerged in a secretive context. The fascination over the players' identities was a fascination with a concealed truth, one that resided behind or beyond the surface of the film. The actor first appeared as the revelation of the mystery of the labor behind filmmaking; the picture personality appeared as the revelation of the "real" names and personalities of the actors; and the star appeared as the revelation of the picture personalities' private identities outside of films. Each of these stages introduced a level of secrecy and truth beneath or beyond the previous one. Thus, the expansion of the player's identity is directly connected to the hermeneutic described earlier; it raised the stakes of the spectator's search for the truth of the actor's identity by extending it or, perhaps more accurately, deepening it. A set of secrets was introduced beneath a set of secrets, *en abyme*. The private finally emerged as the ultimate or most ulterior truth. With each of the three marked expansions of knowledge about the players, the industry provided itself a more elaborate grid through which the actor's identity could be specified and differentiated, and thus a more supple and powerful means of promotion. And with each, the spectator's fascination in the search for the actor's identity was intensified, complicated, and driven forward.

It should not be surprising that a system of discourse driven by a logic of secrecy (and revelation) would light upon the sexual as the ultimate secret—particularly since the truth of the star's identity had already been located in the realm of the private. The star system, and arguably twentieth-century culture in general, depends on an interpretative schema that equates identity with the private and furthermore accords the sexual the status of the most private, and thus the most truthful, locus of identity. Previous chapters noted Foucault's work on the history of sexuality and stressed the similarities between his description of the deployment of the "secret" of sexuality and the deployment of the "secret" of the player's identity. It might be argued that this similarity is merely one of discursive strategy; a logic of secrecy could, after all, be used in discursive fields that otherwise have little in common. But one has to suspect that this similarity involves more than a coincidence of strategy, that the discourses of sexuality and the discourses of stardom are linked in a more fundamental way.

At one level this is all too obvious. The popularity of stars has always been linked with their "sex appeal," and the narrative cinema, practically from its inception, specialized in stories that presented idealized versions of men and women engaged in heterosexual romance. There is no shortage of evidence of fans "falling in love" with these men and women and becoming attached to them in ways that were hardly chaste. But the point here is not merely that the star's appeal is based on his or her sexuality, but that the very modes of knowing the star, of investigating the truth of his or her identity, are linked to and a part of a broader strategy of deploying sexuality in modern times. Foucault's work confines itself largely to the way the discourses of high culture—science, medicine, and literature—worked to constitute ways of speaking sexuality and thus "knowing" it. It is undoubtedly significant that movie stardom, the mass cultural phenomenon par excellence, depends largely on the same ways of speaking and knowing.

Foucault shows how sexuality has been constituted primarily as a problem of truth in modern western society and notes the ways a "will to knowledge" elicited concerning sexuality has led to incessant efforts to uncover its "truth." In the process sexuality has become a particularly privileged site of truth, in some contexts no doubt the ultimate truth. This is certainly the case in the star system. The will to knowledge noted by Foucault aptly describes the fan's intense and insistent involvement in discovering the truth of the star's identity. And, as I hope I have demonstrated, that truth is, at its limit, the truth of sexuality. The sexual scandal is the primal scene of all star discourse, the only scenario that offers the promise of a full and satisfying disclosure of the star's identity.

The will to knowledge about sexuality, Foucault argues, has been supported by two related forms, each of which appears as a crucial component of star discourse. The first is the constitution of the truth of sexuality as a secret. Newspapers and fan magazines similarly constituted the truth of the star's identity as a secret, even as the publicity machine turned out millions of words about the real lives of the stars. That secret was never divorced from the question of sexuality, though it was linked to it more and more explicitly as the star system developed. First, fans "discovered" the secret of the star's real, bodily, existence outside of films, later the secret of the star's married life, and later still, in the twenties, the secret of the star's sexual affairs and transgressions.

The second, interrelated form supporting the will to knowledge of sexuality was, for Foucault, the confession:

> From Christian penance to the present day, sex was a privileged theme of confession. A thing that was hidden, we are told. But what if, on the contrary, it was what, in a quite particular way, one confessed? Suppose the obligation to conceal it was but another aspect of the duty to admit to it (concealing it all the more and with greater care as the confession of it was more important, requiring a stricter ritual and promising more decisive effects)? What if sex in our society, on a scale of several centuries, was something that was placed within an unrelenting system of confession? . . . [It] is in the confession that truth and sex are joined through the obligatory and exhaustive expression of an individual secret.[44]

Foucault is interested here in the ways that rituals of confession (associated historically with religion) have been taken up over the last three centuries by a host of secular institutions—medicine, psychiatry, pedagogy—as the mechanism of "putting sex into discourse," of allowing its "truth" to emerge. The star system, of course, depends heavily on scenes of confession in which the stars, in interviews or in first-person accounts, bare their souls and confess the secrets of their true feelings and their private lives. Examples abound: from "The Confessions of Theda Bara" to "Love Confessions of a Fat Man" (written presumably just before Arbuckle entered into a properly judicial system of confession) to regular items in today's tabloid press and in television interviews conducted by Barbara Walters.[45] The star system then exists in part as a kind of confessional apparatus.

The confessions elicited lead us to the private, and, as I have suggested, the sexual stands as the privileged, ultimate truth of the private.

It is important to be clear here. The player's identity includes other information beyond the sexual, and there is no doubt that our interest in the stars' hobbies and possessions partly accounts for our interest in reading about them and following their films. Yet this hardly accounts for the intensity of our involvement, the fanaticism of the fan. Our sexual attraction to the stars comes closer to accounting for this fanaticism. But I would argue that our involvement in stars is linked not merely to their status as objects of our sexual affection, but to the way the star system engages us in the very processes through which our society constitutes sexuality as an object of knowledge and fascination. The dynamic of secrecy and confession, concealment and revelation that supports discourse on sexuality supports discourse on stars as well. The star system continually sets us out on an investigation, an investigation that is, both in its methods (eliciting confessions and unveiling secrets) and in its promised result (revealing the sexual as the ultimate, ulterior truth of the player's identity), closely tied to the constitution and deployment of sexuality in modern times.

Psychoanalysis and the cinema both emerged at the end of the nineteenth century, and writers in recent years have speculated that this might be something more than a meaningless coincidence. Perhaps these two radical inventions are part of the same history in some deeper sense, symptoms of similar obsessions or perhaps some broad historical shift. Such speculations, interesting as they are, have remained little more than that, dependent primarily on an identification of the surprising commonalities between psychoanalysis and cinema. Raymond Bellour has argued that psychoanalysis and the cinema emerged as the most radical manifestations of a broader shift in subjectivity in the nineteenth century, a subjectivity articulated through a new emphasis on the relation between image production and desire. The role of images is of course central to psychoanalysis as well as the cinema; in fact Freud, in his attempts to explain unconscious dream processes, had recourse to an optical model that much resembles the cinematic apparatus. Bellour and Nick Browne have further noted that both psychoanalysis and early narrative cinema developed around a similar—and a similarly obsessive—vision of the familial dynamic.[46] Though I can do little here but add to these broad speculations, it seems important to at least note the numerous similarities between the cinema's star system and psychoanalysis. Both take identity (or even personality) as their object; both depend upon a model of surface and depth and search for the truth of identity beneath surface manifestations; both look to a private, familial identity to locate that truth, and both assume, furthermore, that that truth is, at its core, sexual. It is undoubtedly significant that these two systems of considering the question of identity should develop more or less simultaneously and share so many preoccupations, particularly if we admit that they have together (though in somewhat distinct domains) so utterly dominated considerations of identity in this century.[47]

The model of surface and depth that has underpinned the expansion of the star system has also, as I have argued, underpinned the spectator's engagement with the star system and with individual stars. A great deal of work has been done on the spectator's engagement with the cinema's signifying processes, but most of this work has followed from the claim that the fundamental determinant of the spectator's engagement is the apparatus, the visual disposition (and a psychological disposition that is often extrapolated from it) of the spectator before the screen. In such work the apparatus (however broadly it is defined) exists primarily as an orientation of visual attention. Jean Louis Baudry, for instance, has argued that the technological base of the cinema (*l'appareil de base*) exists fundamentally as a deployment of the spectator's vision; it works to produce the illusion that the spectator is the transcendental center of the universe and gives the impression that everything exists for his or her sight. Hugo Munsterberg, writing sixty years earlier, offered some comments which, while moving away from the technology of the cinema and more toward its language, support Baudry's basic claim. Munsterberg argued that the codes of film editing function to mimic the "natural" course of the spectator's visual attention. Raymond

Bellour has posited the viewpoint of the camera as the perspective through which both the spectator and the enunciating subject are positioned. And, finally, Stephen Heath has claimed that every film is a dramatization of vision, both of our vision and the vision of the characters that we are aligned with within the story of the film. How, he asks, can one "make sense in film if not through vision, film with its founding ideology of vision as truth."[48] All of these arguments pursue a common point: that the fundamental means of the cinema's engagement of a spectator is through its orientation of visual attention.

The "apparatus" of the star system has been described here as an orientation of the spectator's attention as well, but not essentially a visual orientation. The star system leads us toward that which is behind or beyond the image, hidden from sight. It is in this sense that one can recognize a tension between the optical basis of the cinematic apparatus and that part of it that was put in place with the star system. The former depends on a syntagmatic movement of vision from one shot to the next, the latter on a paradigmatic movement that seeks out the truth concealed behind the images. This may lead us to revise Heath's assessment that the cinema is constantly equating truth and vision: at one level this is obviously correct, but the truth of the star is never more than partially visible; it demands an orientation of attention beyond that which can be simply seen. Of course, it would be ludicrous to suggest that the visual has no place in the star system. Acting is read largely as a manipulation of visual signs, and the star, throughout its history, has existed as an object of visual fascination. The star system is utterly dependent on the orientation of vision that for Baudry and others constitutes the cinematic apparatus. But the star cannot be reduced to this enactment of the spectator's vision.

The star system has, however, inserted itself quite powerfully into a problematic set in place by the technological base of the cinematic apparatus. It has done so not so much through the orientation of vision as through the negotiation of the status of the object seen. The impression of reality that the cinema produces is of course only that—although the objects and events presented in film are present to the eye they are at the same time, and more fundamentally, absent. Of course, all objects within the film are equally absent. The star, however, emerged as a particularly privileged site at which this relationship between presence and absence could be negotiated and turned into a matter of pleasure and fascination. The star system has functioned to "fill in" the lack that constitutes the cinematic signifier and thus to elicit a sense of fullness and presence (however imaginary and fleeting) in place of the absence that is the inevitable consequence of the cinematic apparatus. If, as Walter Benjamin argued, mechanical reproduction results in the loss of the aura of the real object, then the star system might be seen as a peculiar attempt to replace it.[49] That replacement is never fully achieved, however. In effect, the dialectic of presence and absence remains, engaging the spectator in a play of signification that revolves around a series of closely related and often overlapping antimonies—illusion/reality, proximity/distance, public/private, and surface/depth.

One often encounters the claim that the star system fundamentally changed in the second half of this century and that the stars of today are qualitatively different than the stars of old, not as big or as glamorous or as appealing. A number of convincing reasons can be given for such a change—the rise of television, the end of the studio system, the popularization of the auteur theory, the inflation of discourse about personalities from every field, a postmodern flattening of models of depth. There is no doubt some basis (beyond nostalgia) for this claim, and I hope historians will take a careful look at the ways and the reasons the star system of the present differs from that of the past. However, in conducting this study, I have been struck more by the opposite perception—at how little the star system has changed, at how stable the discourses of stardom have been over the last sixty-five years. Although the auteur theory has had an undeniable impact, the star is still viewed as the principal subject of the film's enunciative processes. And our investigation of the identity of that subject is ruled by the same pressures to search out the secret of the star's identity beyond the film into the realms of the private and the sexual. Finally, we still tend to grasp the identity of those who appear in films at relatively distinct levels—as actor (as a professional manipulator of signs), as picture personality (as a personality extrapolated from films), and as star (as someone with a private life distinct from screen image). These levels were developed successively, added one beneath another, through the course of the star system's development between 1907 and 1922. The stars produced during this period have, by and large, faded from popular memory, but the system of discourse that produced them still functions, putting forward new idols and objects of desire, and defining, to a degree that film theory has been reluctant to admit, our experience of cinema.

NOTES

1. "Alan Dales's Intimate Talks with Stage People," *Chicago Herald*, Jan. 3, 1915, unpaginated clipping, New York Public Library Theater Arts Collection (hereafter NYPLTAC).

2. For overviews of the Arbuckle and Taylor scandals see David Y. Yallop, *The Day the Laughter Stopped: The True Story of Fatty Arbuckle* (New York: St. Martin's Press, 1976), and Sidney Kirkpatrick, *A Cast of Killers* (New York: Penguin Books, 1987).

3. *Sunset*, Sept. 1916, p. 32; "The Movie Struck Girl," *Woman's Home Companion*, June 1918, p. 18.

4. *Photoplay*, Oct. 1921, p. 80.

5. Ibid., Nov. 1920, p. 50; June 1921, p. 40.

6. Ibid., July 1920, p. 46. It should be noted that there was a sharp upturn in divorce rates in the United States in the late teens.

7. *New York Times*, Mar. 4, 1920, p. 9.

8. *Photoplay*, Nov. 1917, pp. 35–36.

9. *New York Times*, Mar. 7, 1920, p. 22; *Photoplay*, June 1920, p. 74.

10. *New York Times*, Mar. 31, 1920, p. 1.

11. The "sinister" aspects of this story could have been exacerbated by the Nevada Attorney General's suit, in April 1920, to annul Pickford and Moore's divorce. Pickford had taken an oath that she was a permanent Nevada resident to obtain her divorce. Her move to Los Angeles immediately after the divorce and her marriage to a California resident made her status as a Nevada resident suspect. The charge was that the divorce decree had been "secured as a result of fraud and through collusion between herself [Pickford] and Moore" (*New York Times*, Apr. 4, 1920, p. 1). The case

dragged on and on; the divorce was upheld in June 1921, but the State's appeal to the Nevada Supreme Court delayed a final resolution until 1922. Had the state won the case Pickford would have found herself married to two men.

12. *New York Times*, June 3, 1920, p. 10; June 2, 1920, p. 9.

13. *Photoplay*, June 1920, pp. 70, 73.

14. Ibid., Nov. 1922, p. 27.

15. *Dallas Morning News*, Sept. 12, 1921, p. 1.

16. *Photoplay*, Feb. 1918, p. 70.

17. *Dallas Morning News*, Sept. 12, 1921, p. 1; Sept. 15, 1921, p. 1; Sept. 23, 1921, p. 1.

18. Ibid., Sept. 12, 1921, p. 1.

19. Ibid., Sept. 15, 1921, p. 1.

20. Ibid., Sept. 12, 1921, p. 1; *New York Times*, Dec. 18, 1921, p. 10; *New York Times*, Sept. 15, 1921, p. 10; *Dallas Morning News*, Sept. 15, 1921, p. 1.

21. "Love Confessions of a Fat Man," *Photoplay*, Sept. 1921, p. 22.

22. Ibid., p. 23.

23. Raymond Moley, *The Hays Office* (Indianapolis: Bobbs-Merrill, 1945), p. 27.

24. *Dallas Morning News*, Sept. 15, 1921, p. 1; *New York Times*, Sept. 16, 1921, p. 3; on this point see the unpaginated clipping, *Syracuse Journal*, Sept. 21, 1921, NYPLTAC.

25. Congressional Record, 62:9657, June 29, 1922, as quoted in Moley, p. 27.

26. An undated letter from Will Hays to George Ade in the Will Hays Collection, Indiana State Library, indicates that the original communication was signed by Adolph Zukor, William Fox, Samuel Goldwyn, W. E. Atkinson, Morris Kohn, Rufus Cole, Louis Selznick, P. L. Waters, and Carl Laemmle.

27. *Detroit News*, Jan. 15, 1922, unpaginated clipping, Will Hays Collection.

28. See Moley, *The Hays Office*.

29. This decision was rivaled in fame only by Hays's "reinstatement" of Arbuckle at the end of the year, a public relations blunder made ostensibly in the "spirit of Christmas" and "Christian charity" (Undated press release, MPPDA, Will Hays Collection).

30. Arbuckle agreement, Hays Collection.

31. Telegram to William Fox, Apr. 1, 1922, Hays Collection.

32. Agenda, MPPDA board meeting, Apr. 7, 1922, Hays Collection.

33. George Ade, "Answering Wild-eyed Questions about the Movie Stars at Hollywood," *American Magazine* 93 (May 1922): 52. See also Otis Skinner, "Scandal and the Movies," *Ladies Home Journal* 31 (June 1922): 8. A third article written by Karl Kitchen appeared in *Literary Digest* around this time, offering the following observation about Hollywood: "There is no evidence of any life—wicked or of the night variety—anywhere within its precincts. If in the daytime more than two people walk abreast in Hollywood or Sunset Boulevard—broad avenues that lead nowhere—the inhabitants mistake them for a parade" (June 18, 1922, p. 40).

34. Ade, "Answering Wild-eyed Questions," p. 53.

35. *Photoplay*, Apr. 1922, p. 52; *Literary Digest*, Apr. 1, 1922, p. 33; *Rochester Times Union*, May 2, 1922, NYPLTAC; *New York Telegraph*, Jan. 23, 1923, Will Hays Collection.

36. Will Hays, *The Memoirs of Will H. Hays* (Garden City, N.Y.: Doubleday, 1955), p. 392; *New York Times*, July 30, 1922, NYPLTAC.

37. *Dallas Morning News*, Aug. 10, 1922.

38. Hays, *Memoirs*, p. 392; *Merkimer Telegraph*, Dec. 18, 1922, NYPLTAC.

39. *Washington Times*, Aug. 13, 1922; *Winston-Salem Sentinel*, Aug. 11, 1922; *Norwich Record*, Aug. 10, 1922; *Los Angeles Express*, Aug. 10, 1922; Will Hays Collection.

40. *Merkimer Telegraph*, Dec. 18, 1922, Will Hays Collection.

41. Gilman M. Ostrander, "The Revolution in Morals," in *Change and Continuity in Twentieth Century America: The 1920's*, ed. John Braeman, Robert H. Bremner, and David Brody (Columbus: Ohio State University Press, 1965).

42. It is worth noting the nature of star discourse about the vamps because it demonstrates both the moral uncertainty about them and a desire to keep their image within conventional bounds. An article in 1918 in *Photoplay* (May 1918, p. 82) offered Bara's comments on her morality. "'People write me letters,' she said smilingly; 'and they ask me if I am as wicked as I seem on the screen. I look at my little canary and I say "Dicky, am I so wicked?" And Dicky says, "Tweet, tweet." That may mean "yes, yes," or "no, no," may it not?'" The article is entitled "Does Theda Bara Believe Her Own Press Agent," however, indicating of course that her wicked image

is merely that—an image constructed by a press agent—and that she is really a good, if somewhat confused, person.

A similar example from the same year can be found in an article on vamp Louise Glaum (*Photoplay*, Aug. 1918, p. 33). It is entitled "Vampire or Ingenue?" Thus, it manifests the same sense of uncertainty that the Bara quotation does. However, the subtitle contains a similar reassurance: "Even Louise Glaum's Press Agent Never Learned. However, Who Ever Saw a Siren in a Tam O'Shanter?"

43. *Dallas Morning News*, Sept. 12, 1921, p. 1.

44. Michel Foucault, *The History of Sexuality*, vol. 1, trans. Robert Hurley (New York: Pantheon Books, 1978), p. 63.

45. See *Photoplay*, June 20, 1920, pp. 57–58, and Sept. 1921, p. 22. This system of confession reverses the positions operative in other institutional settings, putting us (the fans) in the privileged position of priest, judge, doctor, psychiatrist, asking us to diagnose, judge, condemn, or forgive. The power relations that underpin the star-spectator relation are obviously not a simple matter of the stars "having" power over us.

46. See "Alternation, Segmentation, Hypnosis: Interview with Raymond Bellour," *Camera Obscura* 3–4, pp. 105–33, and Nick Browne, "Griffith's Family Discourse: Griffith and Freud," *Quarterly Review of Film Studies* 6, no. 1 (Winter 1981): 67–80, also in *Home Is Where the Heart Is: Studies in Melodrama and the Woman's Film*, ed. Christine Gledhill (London: British Film Institute, 1987), pp. 223–35. On the metaphor of the camera obscura in nineteenth-century thought see Sarah Kofman, *Camera obscura de l'idéologie* (Paris: Editions Galilee, 1973).

47. Obviously, more concrete work needs to be done in this area. Such work might take into account Peter Brooks's comments about melodrama and its connections to psychoanalysis; the model of surface and depth he claims is operative in melodrama might apply to related strategies in the star system, particularly if we accept his claim that melodrama provides us with the dominant mode of thinking about the world in modern times. Warren Susman's essay on the concept of personality is also suggestive here. See Peter Brooks, *The Melodramatic Imagination: Balzac, Henry James, Melodrama and the Mode of Excess* (New Haven, Conn.: Yale University Press, 1976), and Warren Susman, "'Personality' and the Making of Twentieth Century Culture," in *Culture as History* (New York: Pantheon Books, 1984).

48. See Jean Louis Baudry, "The Ideological Effects of the Basic Cinematographic Apparatus," trans. Alan Williams, *Film Quarterly* 27 (Winter

1974–75): 39–47, and "The Apparatus," *Camera Obscura* 1 (Dec. 1976): 104–26; Hugo Munsterberg, *The Film: A Psychological Study* (New York: D. Appleton, 1916; reprint, New York: Dover Press, 1970); Raymond Bellour, "Hitchcock the Enunciator," *Camera Obscura* 2 (Fall 1977): 87; Stephen Heath, "Narrative Space," *Screen* 17, no. 3 (Autumn 1976): 91.

49. Walter Benjamin, "The Work of Art in the Age of Mechanical Reproduction," in *Illuminations*, ed. Hannah Arendt, trans. Harry Zohn (New York: Schocken Books, 1978), pp. 217–53.

Bibliography

Ade, George. "Answering Wild-eyed Questions about the Movie Stars at Hollywood." *American Magazine* 93 (May 1922): 52–53.

Affron, Charles. *Star Acting.* New York: E. P. Dutton, 1977.

Allen, Jeanne Thomas. "The Decay of the Motion Picture Patents Company." In *The American Film Industry,* ed. Tino Balio. Madison: University of Wisconsin Press, 1976.

Allen, Robert C. *Vaudeville and Film 1895–1915: A Study in Media Interaction.* New York: Arno Press, 1980.

Balio, Tino, ed. *The American Film Industry.* Madison: University of Wisconsin Press, 1976.

Barthes, Roland. *Camera Lucida.* Trans. Richard Howard. New York: Hill and Wang, 1981.

————. *Image, Music, Text.* Trans. Stephen Heath. New York: Hill and Wang, 1974.

————. "La vedette, enquetes d'audience?" *Communications* 2, 1963: 197–216.

————. *S/Z.* Trans. Richard Howard. New York: Hill and Wang, 1974.

Baudry, Jean Louis. "The Apparatus." *Camera Obscura* 1 (Dec. 1976): 104–26.

————. "The Ideological Effects of the Basic Cinematographic Apparatus." Trans. Alan Williams. *Film Quarterly* 27 (Winter 1974–75): 39–47.

Bellour, Raymond. "Hitchcock the Enunciator." *Camera Obscura* 2 (Fall 1977): 69–94.

Benjamin, Walter. *Illuminations.* Ed. Hannah Arendt. Trans. Harry Zohn. New York: Schocken Books, 1978.

————. "The Work of Art in the Age of Mechanical Reproduction." In

Illuminations, ed. Hannah Arendt. Trans. Harry Zohn. New York: Schocken Books, 1978.

Benveniste, Emile. "L'appareil formel de l'énonciation." *Langages* 17 (Mar. 1970): 12–19.

————. *Problems in General Linguistics.* Trans. M. E. Meek. Coral Gables: University of Miami Press, 1971.

Bergstrom, Janet. "Alternation, Segmentation, Hypnosis: Interview with Raymond Bellour." *Camera Obscura* 3–4 (Summer 1979): 71–103.

Bordwell, David, Janet Staiger, and Kristin Thompson. *The Classical Hollywood Cinema: Film Style and Mode of Production to 1960.* New York: Columbia University Press, 1985.

Brooks, Peter. *The Melodramatic Imagination: Balzac, Henry James, Melodrama and the Mode of Excess.* New Haven, Conn.: Yale University Press, 1976.

Browne, Nick. "Griffith's Family Discourse: Griffith and Freud." *Quarterly Review of Film Studies* 6, no. 1 (Winter 1981). Reprinted in *Home Is Where the Heart Is: Studies in Melodrama and the Woman's Film,* ed. Christine Gledhill. London: British Film Institute, 1987, 223–34.

————. "The Spectator-in-the-Text: The Rhetoric of *Stagecoach.*" *Film Quarterly* 29, no. 2 (Winter 1975–76): 26–38.

Carroll, David. *The Matinee Idols.* London: Peter Owen, 1972.

Caughie, John. *Theories of Authorship.* London: British Film Institute, 1981.

Crofts, Stephen. "Authorship and Hollywood." *Wide Angle* 5, no. 3, (Summer 1983): 16–23.

Dyer, Richard. *Heavenly Bodies: Film Stars and Society.* New York: St. Martin's Press, 1986.

————. *Stars.* London: British Film Institute, 1979.

Eaton, Walter Prichard. "The Canned Drama." *American Magazine* 68 (Sept. 1909): 493–500.

————. "Class Consciousness and the Movies." *The Atlantic Monthly* 115 (Jan. 1915): 48–56.

Ewen, Stuart. *Captains of Consciousness: Advertising and the Social Roots of Mass Culture.* New York: McGraw-Hill, 1976.

Fell, John, ed. *Film before Griffith.* Berkeley: University of California Press, 1983.

Foucault, Michel. *The Archaeology of Knowledge.* Trans. A. M. Sheridan Smith. New York: Harper and Row, 1972.

————. *The History of Sexuality*, vol. 1. Trans. Robert Hurley. New York: Pantheon Books, 1978.

————. "What Is an Author?" In *Textual Strategies: Perspectives in Post-Structuralist Criticism*, ed. Josue V. Harari. Ithaca, N.Y.: Cornell University Press, 1979.

Gledhill, Christine, ed. *Home Is Where the Heart Is: Studies in Melodrama and the Woman's Film*. London: British Film Institute, 1987.

Grau, Robert. *Theatre of Science*. New York: Broadway, 1914.

Griffith, Richard. *The Movie Stars*. New York: Doubleday, 1970.

Gunning, Thomas R. "D. W. Griffith and the Narrator-System: Narrative Structure and Industry Organization In Biograph Films, 1908–1909." Ph.D. diss., New York University, 1986.

————. *D. W. Griffith and the Origins of American Narrative Film: The Early Years at Biograph*. Urbana: University of Illinois Press, forthcoming.

Hampton, Benjamin. *A History of the Movies*. New York: Covici, Friede, 1931. Reprinted as *History of the American Film Industry*. New York: Dover Books, 1970.

Harari, Josue V., ed. *Textual Strategies: Perspectives in Post-Structuralist Criticism*. Ithaca, N.Y.: Cornell University Press, 1979.

Hays, Will. *The Memoirs of Will H. Hays*. Garden City, N.Y.: Doubleday, 1955.

Hays, Will, Collection, Indiana State Library.

Heath, Stephen. "Narrative Space." *Screen* 17, no. 3 (Autumn 1976): 68–113.

Holman, Roger, ed. *Cinema 1900–1906: An Analytical Study*. Brussels: Federation Internationale des Archives du Film, 1982.

Jacobs, Lewis. *The Rise of the American Film: A Critical History*. New York: Harcourt, Brace, 1939.

Jowett, Garth. *Film: The Democratic Art*. Boston: Little, Brown, 1976.

Kindem, Gorham. "Hollywood's Movie Star System: A Historical Overview." In *The American Movie Industry: The Business of Moving Pictures*, ed. Gorham Kindem. Carbondale: Southern Illinois University Press, 1982.

————, ed. *The American Movie Industry: The Business of Moving Pictures*. Carbondale: Southern Illinois University Press, 1982.

Kirkpatrick, Sidney. *A Cast of Killers*. New York: Penguin Books, 1987.

Kitchell, William H. "The Artists of the Screen." *Moving Picture World*, Sept. 30, 1911, 949.

Klumph, Inez, and Helen Klumph. *Screen Acting: Its Requirements and Rewards.* New York: Falk, 1922.

Kofman, Sarah. *Camera obscura de l'idéologie.* Paris: Editions Galilee, 1973.

Kohansky, Mendel. *The Disreputable Profession: The Actor in Society.* Westport, Conn.: Greenwood Press, 1984.

La Place, Maria. "Bette Davis and the Ideal of Consumption." *Wide Angle* 6, no. 4, (Fall 1984): 34–44.

Lawrence, Florence, Collection, Los Angeles County Museum of Natural History.

Leyda, Jay, and Charles Musser. *Before Hollywood.* New York: American Federation of the Arts, 1986.

Lounsbury, Myron. *The Origins of American Film Criticism.* New York: Arno Press, 1973.

Lowenthal, Leo. *Literature, Popular Culture and Society.* Englewood Cliffs, N.J.: Prentice-Hall, 1961.

————. "The Triumph of Mass Idols." In *Literature, Popular Culture, and Society,* ed. Leo Lowenthal. Englewood Cliffs, N.J.: Prentice-Hall, 1961.

McArthur, Benjamin. *Actors and American Culture, 1880–1920.* Philadelphia: Temple University Press, 1984.

McLaughlin, R. G. *Broadway and Hollywood: A History of Economic Interaction.* New York: Arno Press, 1961.

Marsh, Mae. *Screen Acting.* Los Angeles: Photo-star Publishing, 1921.

Mast, Gerald. *A Short History of the Movies.* Indianapolis: Bobbs-Merrill, 1976.

May, Lary. *Screening Out the Past: The Birth of Mass Culture and the Motion Picture Industry.* New York: Oxford University Press, 1980.

Mayne, Judith. "Immigrants and Spectators." *Wide Angle* 5, no. 2 (1982): 32–40.

Metz, Christian. *The Imaginary Signifier.* Trans. Celia Britton, Annsyl Williams, Ben Brewster, and Alfred Guzzetti. Bloomington: Indiana University Press, 1982.

Moley, Raymond. *The Hays Office.* Indianapolis: Bobbs-Merrill, 1945.

Morin, Edgar. *The Stars.* New York: Grove Press, 1966.

Munsterberg, Hugo. *The Film: A Psychological Study.* New York: D. Appleton, 1916. Reprint, New York: Dover Press, 1970.

Musser, Charles. "Another Look at the 'Chaser Theory.'" *Studies in Visual Communication* 10, no. 4 (Fall 1984): 24–44.

————. "The Nickelodeon Era Begins: Establishing the Framework for Hollywood's Mode of Representation." *Framework* 22–23 (Autumn 1983): 4–11.

North, Joseph H. *The Early Development of the Motion Picture 1887–1909.* New York: Arno Press, 1973.

Ostrander, Gilman M. "The Revolution in Morals." In *Change and Continuity in Twentieth Century America: The 1920's,* ed. John Braeman, Robert H. Bremner, and David Brody. Columbus: Ohio State University Press, 1965.

Pearson, Roberta. "'The Modesty of Nature': Performance Style in the Griffith Biographs." Ph. D. diss., New York University, 1987.

————, and William Uricchio. *Invisible Viewers, Inaudible Voices: Intertextuality and Reception in the Early Cinema.* Princeton, N.J.: Princeton University Press, forthcoming.

Poggi, Jack. *Theater in America: The Impact of Economic Forces, 1870–1967.* Ithaca, N.Y.: Cornell University Press, 1968.

Ramsaye, Terry. *A Million and One Nights: A History of the Motion Picture Industry.* New York: Simon and Schuster, 1964.

Sargent, Epes Winthrop. "Advertising for Exhibitors." *Moving Picture World,* Oct. 21, 1911.

Schickel, Richard. *His Picture in the Papers.* New York: Charterhouse, 1974.

————. *The Stars.* New York: Bonanza Books, 1962.

See, Carolyn Penelope. "The Hollywood Novel: An Historical and Critical Study." Ph.D. diss., University of California, Los Angeles, 1963.

Skinner, Otis. "Scandal and the Movies." *Ladies Home Journal* 32 (June 1922): 8.

Sklar, Robert. *Movie-made America: A Cultural History of the Movies.* New York: Vintage Books, 1976.

Slide, Anthony. *Aspects of American Film History Prior to 1920.* Metuchen, N.J.: Scarecrow Press, 1978.

————. *The Big V: A History of the Vitagraph Company.* Metuchen, N.J.: Scarecrow Press, 1976.

————. "The Evolution of the Film Star." In *Aspects of American Film History Prior to 1920,* ed. Anthony Slide. Metuchen, N.J.: Scarecrow Press, 1978.

Smoodin, Eric. "Attitudes of the American Printed Medium toward the Cinema: 1894–1908." Unpublished paper, University of California, Los Angeles, 1979.

Souriau, Etienne. *L'univers filmique*. Paris: Flammarion, 1953.

Staiger, Janet. "The Eyes Really Are the Focus: Photoplay Acting and Film Form and Style." *Wide Angle* 6, no. 4 (Fall 1984): 14–24.

———. "Seeing Stars." *Velvet Light Trap* 20 (Summer 1983): 10–15.

Susman, Warren. *Culture as History*. New York: Pantheon Books, 1984.

———. "'Personality' and the Making of Twentieth Century Culture." In *Culture as History*, ed. Warren Susman. New York: Pantheon Books, 1984.

Volosinov, V. N. *Marxism and the Philosophy of Language*. Trans. Ladisav Matejak and I. R. Titunik. New York: Seminar Press, 1973.

Walker, Alexander. *Stardom: The Hollywood Phenomenon*. New York: Stein and Day, 1970.

Woods, Frank E. "Why Is a Star?" *Photoplay*, Nov. 1919.

Yallop, David Y. *The Day the Laughter Stopped: The True Story of Fatty Arbuckle*. New York: St. Martin's Press, 1976.

Index

players' appearance at Republic
Theater, 80–81; mentioned, 44, 52
Intertextuality. *See* Star system

Jacobs, Lewis, 4

Kalem, 5, 8, 40, 52
Kerrigan, Warren, 73
Kindem, Gorham, 5

Labor, role of in production of films,
29–32, 46, 78–81
Laemmle, Carl: in previous histories,
2–6; and early promotions, 55–62;
criticized by Grau, 80–81;
mentioned, 8
Lawrence, Florence: in previous
histories, 2–6; Imp promotion, 55–
62; and Lubin, 62–63; specificity of
image, 73; mentioned, 10, 23, 44,
50, 52, 70
Leonard, Marion, 67–70, 82–83, 105
Lepanto, Victoria, 38, 54
Lubin Manufacturing Company, 62–
63

Metz, Christian, 14–18
Moore, Owen, 70, 72, 105, 121–24
Morality clauses, 133–34
Motion Picture Patents Company, 2–
3, 8, 26, 59, 78
Motion Picture Producers and
Distributors Association, 129–36

Names: concealment of, 7, 77–85;
circulation of, 20; as site of
fascination and knowledge, 73–85;
and cast lists, 75–76

Otis, Elita Proctor, 41

Pathé, 36–40, 54
Pickford, Mary: in previous histories,
2–4; and Famous Players, 45, 71–
72; and Imp, 62, 70–71; at
Biograph, 71; and the "Little Mary"

series, 89; in *Stella Maris*, 110–12;
1915 columns, 113–14; divorce and
remarriage, 121–24, 147; mentioned,
10, 23, 105
Picture personality: mode of existence
in discourse, 73–92; defined, 50–53
Pilar-Morin, 43–44, 50, 51–52, 54
Psychoanalysis. *See* Star system

Ramsaye, Terry, 2–3
Rappe, Virginia. *See* Arbuckle, Roscoe
Reid, Wallace, 117–18, 136

Scandal: potential of, 104, 118–20;
and Arbuckle, 124–32; and divorces
of stars, 119–24; and shift in star
discourse with, 128–29
Secret, knowledge of players as, 77,
80–85, 139–46
Selig, 40
Slide, Anthony, 5, 77
Spooner, Cecil, 8, 42–43
Star: distinguished from picture
personality, 98, 101; distinguished
from theatrical actors, 102–5; and
potential for scandal, 104, 108–20;
family discourse and, 105–7, 123–
24; and consumerism, 107–10, 138–
89; hobbies of, 109; politics and,
110; shifting levels of identity and,
110–12; sexuality and, 141–44. *See
also* Scandal; Secret, knowledge of
players as
Star system: previous histories of, 1–8;
and film as commodity, 7, 11, 28–
30, 46, 78, 110, 112–13; and
individual star, 9–11; defined, 9–13;
and enunciation, 11, 13–21, 39, 46,
80, 110–12; and intertextuality, 12,
16, 18, 20–21, 50–51, 85–90, 90–
92; and textuality of individual film,
110–12; psychoanalysis, 143–44, 150

Taylor, William Desmond, 117–18
Theatrical actors: in film, 24, 36–45;
private lives of, 102